A
TRUE
RELATION

OF THAT HONORABLE, THOUGH UNFORTUNATE

EXPEDITION
OF

KENT, ESSEX,

AND

COLCHESTER,

IN 1648.

CONTAINING

BY MATTHEW CARTER,
QUARTER-MASTER-GENERAL IN THE KING'S FORCES,
ONE AMONG THE PRISONERS WHO SURRENDERED THEMSELVES.

COLCHESTER:
PRINTED AND SOLD BY J. FENNO,
BOOKSELLER AND BINDER, OPPOSITE THE GEORGE, HIGH-STREET;
SOLD ALSO BY SCATCHERD AND WHITAKER, AVE-MARIA-LANE, LONDON.
1788.

i

'Starvation or Surrender'
Has been published
as a Limited Edition of which this is

Number   134.

A list of the original subscribers
is printed at the back of the book.

'STARVATION OR SURRENDER'

Presented by
JOHN HEDGES & PATRICK DENNEY

The SIEGE of COLCHESTER By the Lord Fairfax, As it was with the Line and Outworks 1648

JMH Publications

First published in 2002 by John Hedges & Patrick Denney,

JMH Publications
Ash Road, Alresford, Colchester, Essex, CO7 8DU.

ISBN 0 953063313

Limited edition 500 hardback copies.

Typesetting and Reprographics by Lazertype, Colchester.

Printed and bound by Bath Press, Bath

This book is dedicated to Deirdre and Brian Norman of Mount Bures, Essex, without whose assistance this publication would have been difficult.

Front and Back Cover: Troops marching past Colchester Moot Hall.
by Charles Debenham, Courtesy Colchester Museum Service.

Contents

Illustrations

Frontpiece: Troops Marching Past Old Moot Hall, Colchester

Acknowledgements

My most sincere thanks are extended to Patrick Denney, local historian, and David Clark for their valuable support in this project. My thanks are also extended to the following individuals and organisations that have provided me with valuable assistance in the preparation of this book for publication.

Deirdre and Brian Norman; John and Caryl Gardner; Valerie Sach; Andrew Phillips, local historian; Charles Debenham; Dorothy and Jim Waller; Richard Shackle; Alec Corton; Beryl and Eric Jordan; Fred Salmon; Ruth and Adrian Street; Essex Record Office, Colchester; Colchester and Essex Museum Services; Cultural Activities Committee; Colchester Borough Council; St. Giles Masonic Association; Colchester Masonic Hall Company Ltd; Sir George Lisle's Regiment of the Sealed Knot Society; Lucas and Lisle Lodge, No. 8456; Mr. D.C. Warden; The Reverend Fred Woods, St. Peter's Church, Colchester; Friends of Colchester Archaeology Trust; Friends of Colchester Museums; The Essex Society for Family History; Essex County Libraries, Local Studies Section; Colchester Civic Society; Colchester Recalled Oral History Group.

If there are any omissions to the above list, it is with regret and in no way intentional.

Foreword by
Sir William Boulton Bt., Kt., C.B.E., TD.

In February 2002 I was approached by John Hedges and invited to write a foreword to his new book 'Starvation or Surrender', an invitation that I greatly appreciated, with some doubt, however, as to whether or not there was anything I could usefully contribute to the project. Having read the transcript and obtained some further information from John, I offer the following comments.

For most of my life I have lived fairly close to the town of Colchester and not unnaturally am interested in its history of which the siege is an outstanding episode (although this seems to have attracted very little publicity).

Our present home takes its name from the surrounding woodland, 'the Quarters House' which was extended by the architect Richard Wood to create a folly in 1772, and later painted by landscape artist John Constable in 1816. There is a story that its origin was the quartering of troops here by one side or the other in 1648. This is indeed possible because there is both cover in the woods and also, water; but unfortunately there is nothing in the narrative to support this theory.

It will be apparent to anyone who has read so far that the book is written in the style and language prevailing in the Shakespearian period which calls for a little concentration in regard, for example to the meaning of a sentence here or there, a strange word or the specific site of a particular battle; but the reward for this is a perfectly clear and compelling story of endurance, courage, and loyalty on the part of both of the defending forces and the civilian population, but, mayhem by undisciplined roundhead troops and the ruthlessness of General Fairfax.

A feature of the fighting of special interest to me was prompted by the recollection that during the first siege of Tobruk in 1941 (relieved after 242 days) the Germans scattered leaflets from the air onto the garrison to the effect that it would be annihilated and could only find safety in surrender. It is clear that 350 years earlier, General Fairfax had exactly the same idea as Field Marshal Rommel because a similar message was conveyed to the Royalists by arrows shot into the town wrapped with paper slips; in this case, the response of the bold defenders was to return the arrows with a surprising reply.

The finale is a riveting description of the execution of Sir Charles Lucas and Sir George Lisle, which I feel even after three centuries, could still prompt a tear or lump in the throat.

To turn now from the narrative to the author, Matthew Carter, a quartermaster-general and staunch royalist, and himself taken prisoner who penned the original manuscript for this book for which the title 'Starvation or Surrender' is aptly named.

In 1789 the manuscript was reprinted and sold by J. Fenno of Colchester. This version has now been reproduced by John Hedges who has written two other books and is well known to residents in the village of Alresford and Colchester. 'Starvation or Surrender' should bring about a new awareness of Colchester's history and especially the civil war and siege.
John Hedges, having read the original account was so inspired and fascinated that he felt compelled to revive its contents with much additional information for the present readers assistance.

I commend this publication to you and hope you will enjoy its contents as much as the author and myself.

William Boulton

Preface to this Edition by
Patrick Denney

The Siege of Colchester is one of the best-documented accounts of the entire English Civil War. It was certainly the major event of the so-called second Civil War of 1648 following a determined uprising by a large number of Royalists in Kent who subsequently crossed the Thames and settled themselves in the town of Colchester. For Colchester's part, this was very much a cruel chance of fate for previous to this the town had escaped from any involvement in the fighting. In fact, during the earlier years of the war the town had positioned itself squarely on the side of Parliament and now being obliged to play host to a large Royalist force must have proved a bitter pill to swallow.

The event itself was remarkable for its variety of circumstance. Its long continuance, the strength and determination of both forces, individual heroics and sufferings and the final act of retribution and vengeance, all the components of which modern movie blockbusters are made of. The suffering experienced by the beleaguered townspeople was particularly manifested in the extreme shortage of food and supplies which increased in severity as the siege moved into its final stages. Hundreds of horses were slaughtered to feed the people and many were also reduced to eating cats, dogs, various vermin as well as mutton fat candles. In fact, according to Matthew Carter's account, half of the side of a small dog was selling on the streets of Colchester for six shillings - approximately £25 in today's money. Apparently, it had been decided to kill the cats and dogs first so they would not prey on the rats and mice which were reserved for the poorer people. As well as having to cope with the continual pangs of hunger, the people were also subjected to various forms of plunder, beatings, rape and even murder. Added to this, nearly 200 of their homes were destroyed and trade in the town brought to a virtual standstill.

As it stands, very few eyewitness accounts of the event have survived and of those that have, the most extensive is that recorded by Matthew Carter, a quartermaster general in the King's forces, and the author of the work here presented. Matthew Carter was apparently a gentleman of some standing and influence in Kent and had played a significant part in the Kentish uprising earlier in the year before the army had marched on Colchester. When the town finally surrendered after the 11-week siege, he was one of the 3,530 royalist troops taken prisoner. During his subsequent period of confinement he wrote his version of the action, of which he had been an eyewitness. It was entitled, 'A True Relation of that Honorable, Though Unfortunate Expedition of Kent, Essex, and Colchester in 1648'.

The book was first printed in London in 1650 and later reprinted at various times during the 18th century. This present and largely facsimile version is based on the 1789 edition which was printed and published by J.Fenno of Colchester. The original text has been retained throughout with just a few minor alterations here and there for the sake of clarity. The typeface and layout have also been adjusted to fit in better with a more modern format.

Although Carter's account is comprehensive and remarkably detailed, it is nevertheless written from a Royalist perspective and as such expresses the particular sympathies and biases of its author. Some caution is needed therefore when making any particular judgements regarding its value and reliability. On the positive side, however, one must remember that the author himself was a participant of the action and not therefore forced to rely on second hand or heresy evidence. In fact, it can be argued that Carter gives a very fair assessment of events and one which would be of extreme value to a student of the Civil War.

And so to this present edition, 'Starvation or Surrender' and its ultimate value as an addition to the already existing plethora of books on the Siege of Colchester. Well firstly, it makes freely available an important and relatively scarce source which can usually only be found on the shelves of the local library, or at a high premium in a second-hand bookshop. And secondly, unlike the original edition in which the text can prove a little difficult to navigate one's way through, this version comes complete with a comprehensive index, a biographical section dealing with the leading characters, a daily diary of events, a glossary, numerous illustrations and a large format detachable siege map. All in all, a valuable addition to the library of the committed historian and general reader alike.

Patrick Denney

ADVERTISEMENT

HAVING been repeatedly importuned by a great number of friends in Colchester and its environs, to reprint that scarce and valuable work, **THE SIEGE OF COLCHESTER;** I am at this time induced to bring it forward, not doubting but every encouragement will be given to a subject so interesting. And as the Editor flatters himself his highest ambition has ever been to please, he trusts the revival of this work will receive such encouragement as will perpetuate the memory of that honourable, though unfortunate event.

I am your most devoted
      Humble servant,

The Editor.

THE

PREFACE.

CANDID READER,

I HERE present you with a tragic Relation, limned to the life, being the sacrifice of a Peer of the Realm, and two Gentlemen of eminent rank and quality, faithful Servants to a distressed Master; such as never appeared nor approved themselves more, than when his necessities importuned them most; nor at any time more active, than when hopes of rewards presented them least.

Their task was principally undertaken for the good and vindication of our nation, and such foreign countries, as in these our times of sedition, when

Division is the only musical note which sounds harmoniously in the ears of our Zimries, have thrown aspersions on our nation, of being universally disloyal, may, by the portrait or draught of these, ingeniously confess, that England brings forth heroic and loyal spirits, as well as inferior birds of prey.

For, there is not that state nor age, which can produce persons for action more daring; nor in the conduct of their designs, more discerning; nor any who made a more loyal conclusion.

It were then to be wished, that those who were authors or actors in their fall, would think of their own deplorable condition, that by proper reflections on their worth and excellency, a remorse may be wrote in them for their injuriously inflicted wrath; to which, a desire of revenge and thirst after blood gave heat; and which can be cooled by incessant rivulets of penitential tears only; which done, charity will with, that the infamy of that fact, may be in the same capacity of dying, as the perpetuity of the same of these Royalists, is, with all succeeding posterities of living.

Noble actions, having relation to persons of quality, have been ever memorable to posterity; amongst which, none more remarkable than such as have borne the face of Loyalty, and expressed their true native lustre, in defence of the just privileges of their country, and conservation of a monarchial sovereignty.

Many indeed, and those singular heroic spirits, (whose names are to this day recorded in the Annals of Fame) do our ancient historians present unto us, who have received no other gratuity than ingratitude, from those parts where they have best deserved.

Carthage may satisfy you with an Hannibal, Rome with an African, Athens with a Phocion. Notwithstanding all this, the memory of their surviving actions, begot such a glorious emulation in their successors, as that unthankful-ness their countries shewed unto them, or aspersions which immeriting spirits darted on them, even redounded more to their honour, than if they had never suffered under the censure of a groundless popular opinion, or been crushed by the votes of such statecommanding imperialists, who maligned their rising.

I shall not labour to make any large porch to my Mindian Building, lest some critic tax me, as that Cynic did, that the city might run out at the gate.

We are here to offer to your view and disinterested judgment, equally poised to their merits, Persons of Quality, and Patterns of Loyalty, who have acted their parts bravely upon the theatre of honour; whose names (though the memories of some men be apt to freeze in these distempered times) shall, like fresh and fragrant odours, breathe sweetness in the nostrils of those, who hold fidelity to be the best cognizance for the coat of a subject.

The principle scene of action was at Colchester, than which place, none more memorable for continuance of a Siege beyond expectation; nor more gallant in opposing of a powerful foe with a constant and cheerful resistance.

During which Siege, it is incredible in what a prudential way and form of discipline, those who were designed commanders and managers of this weighty action behaved themselves; not only in animating those who had declared for them, but ingratiating those (and that in a generous manner) of whose afflictions they were doubtful. But to omit the relation of these particulars, (which deserve approval and invitation from those who stand engaged in actions of like quality) we will make it our work to acquaint you more punctually with the descent, breeding and condition of these eminent persons, who closed the sundry passages of their loyal lives, with a glorious evening, by sacrificing their blood for the honour of their sovereign, and endeavouring to ease their oppressed country of an insupportable tyrannic burthan.

First then, for the family of Sir Charles Lucas, none that knows it can bestow any other style upon it, than of lineal worth and antiquity; stem from whence sprung many eminent branches, which proved useful instruments to their state and country; amongst which, this noble Gentleman confers such an addirament upon it, as the loyalty and memory of his person, shall, to succeeding times highly improve.

For his education, it was generous, having his youth sufficiently seasoned in principles of knowledge, human and divine learning; his manhood for discipline in the field; he was ever of an active disposition, accompanied with a resolute spirit, and a suitable discretion to manage it; strict in his commands, without a supercilious severity; free in his rewards to persons of desert and quality. On the first beginning of the distractions of those times, all his expressions, (with whatever company he consorted) ever tended to the advancement of loyalty;

setting forth, how odious and unjustifiable it was to lift up a hand against the power of sovereignty, and would often say, "He preferred the style of Loyalty before any dignity which could be conferred upon him in this world." In his society, he was affable and pleasant; in his charge, serious and vigilant; remiss in nothing that might any way improve or expedite his dispatch in affairs of government. Those of his sundry fields, martial exploits, and brave adventures, wherein he was ever personally engaged, and wherein he usually appeared at the head of the army, as was observed, were needless to recount

As his valor was well known, so was his native candor and clemency no less approved by all such as in the close of his conquest submitted themselves to his mercy; so as, in this particular, we may truly conclude, that during all his time of service, he was ever ready to afford what himself could not receive, free quarter; no, not so much as one day's reprieve to prepare himself for his last voyage.

This is taken notice of here, on purpose to vindicate his clear and noble temper, from the injurious censure of those, who in the freedom of their report, charge him with being too violent and implacable in affairs of this kind; whereas, to say the truth, that man breathes not, who can justly accuse him, in the whole course of his actions or commands, with having laid his impetuous hand upon a submissive captive in cold blood; or ever suffered any blood to be spilt, which he might with honor or without prejudice to his commands spare.

But these Critic Spirits, who are so apt to censure and traduce the clearest actions of honour, may be properly compared to the Chameleon, who can assume any colour but white.

But a Foe must have something to say in his own defence; yet, when he has produced all the reasons he can possibly allege, to wind up the spider-woven web of his apology, he must appear to the whole world, and succeeding posterities after these times of distraction, an actor of a cruel and bloody tragedy. In a word, never did a more undaunted spirit harbor more noble compassion; deeming nothing more inglorious, than to domineer over the misery of a subdued enemy.

Sir George Lisle bore as excellent a character as his friend, companion, brother officer, and fellow sufferer, Sir Charles Lucas; and to bestow on them any ampler character, or present them in a fuller portraiture, would be giving beams to the glorious body of the sun; their integrity being impaled with such honour, as far surmounted the reach of censure.

The Right Honourable the Lord Capell, who was concerned with the two gentlemen before-mentioned in defence of the royal cause, and who also lost his life for the same, and had his vast estate sequestered, was son and heir to Sir Arthur Capell, of Hadham Hall, in Hertfordshire, a gentleman of a great estate. His Lordship had a generous education, and in the happy times of peace, none was more pious, charitable and munificent; in our unhappy differences, none more resolute, loyal and active. The King esteemed him much, and created him a peer. He was a grave and discreet person, and was greatly beloved by the people; he was as good in all his private relations, as in his several public capacities. In the unfortunate differences betwixt the King and Parliament, he constantly and faithfully adhered to his Majesty, and declared openly in the House of Lords, "That his Majesty had granted so much for the peace and security of the kingdom, "that they who asked more, intended the disturbance of it."

He cheerfully engaged in the war, and advanced to his Majesty twelve thousand pounds in money and plate, and between eight and nine hundred horse.

But I shall now hasten to the pursuit of the promised Relation; in doing which, I sincerely assure you, great care is taken to assert truths only; and in the whole work, I have digressed as little as possible, but confined myself to a strict commentary of the real passages; and, to add more to your satisfaction, I have drawn the beginning of this affair, not only from the first step of its motion, but the cause which produced that motion; and which, I hope, will not be displeasing to you.

YOURS,

Matthew Carter.

King Charles I.

The South West view of Colchester Castle, 18th Century

The North East view of Colchester Castle, 18th Century

A

TRUE RELATION

OF THE

SIEGE OF COLCHESTER.

O N Christmas Day, 1647, many gentlemen, and others of meaner rank, in the city of Canterbury in Kent, being religiously disposed to the service of Almighty God, according to the liturgy and orders of the Church of England, (a heinous offence in those times of reformation) met at St. Andrews Church in the High-Street, where the Reverend Mr. Allday, then resident minister of the parish, preached a sermon suitable to the day, a thing then so much out of use, that the people began to forget that Christ was ever born, as well as the celebration of his birth.

This piece of orderly and Christian devotion, startled the consciences of the new saints, who, inflamed with fiery zeal, began to make tumults in the streets, and under the church windows, thinking thereby to drown the voice of the preacher; but it did not discourage him, for he persisted in his holy and devout exercise till the sermon was ended; after which, the people began to flock more tumultuously together, and the disturbance increased very much.

The Mayor of Canterbury (a person knave enough, and I think as much fool, as appears by his conduct) walked through the streets, and endeavoured to prevail on several people to open their shops, and expose their wares to sale in the market place, it being Saturday, and market-day there. One tradesman in particular whom he applied to, answering his worship in such expressions as he could not relish, he struck him a blow in the face with his fist; by which means

1

he made himself the first engager and instrument in the breach of that peace, which he had, upon all occasions, sworn to see kept and preserved.

This occasioned a greater distraction and uproar in the city; considerable numbers thronged together, and growing mad, the Mayor's heels were soon flung up, and his worship thrown in the kennel; after which, he was glad to shift for his life as well as he could. Then one Huse, a constable, (by trade a shoe-maker) a ringleader of the faction, ran hastily up and down the streets with a pistol in his hand, summoning out his crew with aggravating clamors, who, tumbling out of their houses with fire-arms, and other offensive weapons in their hands, beat down and overpowered all they met with; amongst the rest, one White, a barber, (a man swelled as full of ungodly schismatical principles of rebellion, as a toad with poison) standing in the street with a musquet loaded and cocked, and a person whom he knew to be of a different way of thinking from himself, coming to the door, to enquire the cause of the tumult, he let fly at him, and shot him through the body, and there remained small hopes of life in him.

Thus the disorder increased, as is generally the consequence of such mutinous broils. But at length those gentlemen who were most forward in the disturbance, began to slacken in their courage, and gladly betook themselves to their heels, every one shifting for himself; and White being apprehended, was committed to the town goal, there to remain till he should be punished as the law directs for so horrid a villainy.

The other party being enraged and incensed by so foul an affront, began to prepare for their own security; and, well knowing the malice of those they had to deal with, seized on the magazine of the town, and placed guards at every gate of the city, fearing the mischief which afterwards came to pass, though it might have been prevented, had they not thought themselves too secure.

Their numbers being vastly increased, and becoming violent, Sir William Mann, Mr. Lovelace, a councillor, and several other gentlemen, by their extraordinary industry, persuaded them to desist from prosecuting those rash designs which they had boldly resolved on; engaging themselves, jointly with the Mayor, and Mr. Alderman Savine, a justice of the peace, by articles drawn up and signed by them, declaring, that no man should be molested or questioned for any thing which had been done.

Upon this, they all quietly laid down their arms, and every person betook himself to his vocation and particular habitation, which might otherwise have produced greater effects, both in that city and the whole county.

About a month after, upon the instigation of the Mayor, (whose malice could not be appeased without revenge) by order of Parliament, came down Colonel Huson's regiment of foot from about London, to quarter in Canterbury; who were no sooner settled in their quarters, but an order from the Parliament House, they seized on Sir William Mann, Mr. Lovelace, Mr. Savine, Mr. Dudley Wiles, and several other gentlemen, whom they hurried away to Leeds Castle near Maidstone, where they were kept prisoners upwards of two months, till some of the poorer sort, (who had not wherewithal to subsist, none daring to relieve them) were almost starved, as were their wives and families at home.

At length, (after solicitations of the Gentlemen of the House, by the intercession of the Burgesses of the City, and the Deputy Lieutenants of the County, who began to be a little touched with a sense of their abominable injury) so much favour was obtained, as to have bail taken for their liberty, till they should be called upon to answer at the Bar of their mock Justice, for this high and unpardonable riot of peace-making.

This great favour being procured, they all went home; but were scarce settled, before the Mayor, by virtue of his own power, (having Myrmidon's enough at hand to maintain him in any thing, though never so ignoble, wicked or unjust, and notwithstanding his having before signed the Articles of Indemnity, and the sufferings of those poor people) would have had all those of inferior rank to be whipped, or ride the wooden horse; for he knew how to domineer, and had the soldiers to clap him on the back, and encourage whatever he undertook; but, by the grave advice of some of his more moderate brethren, he laid aside that project, and the business lay quiet till about a fortnight before Whitsuntide; at which time, the Parliament gave commission of special Oyer and Terminer for a Court of Sessions in the Castle of Canterbury, and sent thither Sergeant Wild and Sergeant Steel, to try them upon life and death, who, in the whole affair, were the only sufferers; whilst the raisers of the riot, got either to be their judges or witnesses against them to condemn them. Condemned indeed beforehand, as by the sequel appears.

A grand jury of gentlemen was also summonsed in from every lathe of the county, and none pricked but such as they thought so well affected to the Parliament, as to cast any person whom they were desirous should be convicted. All the Deputy Lieutenants were likewise appointed to meet at this great sessions; Sir Michael Lusey, then one of the House, and not in command, (some time before a colonel in the service, and before that, in debt far beyond what he was worth, but at that instant clear from all, and his estate much augmented) applied to the Parliament, for leave to be upon the bench, which was soon granted; and coming to Canterbury, boastingly said, "That he thanked God he had obtained leave of the House to be there; and that he would endeavour to send some of the gentlemen packing to another world." Which he certainly would have done, had God given so large a power into his hands; but his protection guarded them from the ruin intended for them by their unjust judges.

The day being come, and the Judges and Bench seated in the usual state, the Prisoners were summoned to the bar, and the Jury impaneled; after which, the indictment was read, and pleaded against, and the Jury sent out to bring in their verdict, and after duly considering the affair, found an Ignoramus upon it; and being again ordered out, returned with the same verdict. This surprised the Bench, and the Judges were much displeased, having before agreed upon their doom; however, the affair was finished for that time, and the Court broke up, the Judges being in a manner forced so to do, but refused to acquit the Prisoners till they heard further from the Parliament, intending to have brought them to a second trial.

Before the Bench could rise, a packet was brought in from the Parliament House, with a relation of the great defeat given the Welsh at St. Fagons, near Cardiff in Glamorgan shire; which being read, one of the Bench rose up and said to a Gentleman of the Grand Jury, "Had we known this news before, we would have made you have found something else than an Ignoramus; to which the gentleman, being a man of resolution and conscience, made this reply; "Sir, neither your news nor your threatening words, should have compelled us to give in a verdict upon another man's life, contrary to the result of our consciences."

Hereby the world may judge of the justice of those men, whom nothing but fear could keep from committing homicide and murder on their fellow christians, subjects and countrymen, upon the seats of justice and judgment.

After this, all the Grand Jury met together, being vastly displeased at the above unreasonable speech, and discoursed of the intolerable misery and slavery this wretched kingdom was involved and plunged into; and under what a tyranny they now suffered, by the unlimited, usurped and arbitrary jurisdiction their fellow subjects exercised over them, as so many illegal lords and kings; being supported in their proceedings by the unmerciful power of the blood-thirsty sword; disputing with much resolution and boldness among themselves, which way to proceed in order to get free from such inhuman slavery and insufferable bondage; they at length unanimously resolved to petition both Houses of Parliament once more, and endeavour to persuade them to take into consideration, the misery with which they had overwhelmed this gasping common wealth. Accordingly, a Petition was drawn up, and after being corrected, was shown to some of the Deputy Lieutenants, who observing the gentlemen to be resolute in it, dare not disapprove thereof, though at the same time they were sensible it was quite against their interest.

An exact copy of the said Petition follows.

To the Right Honorable the Lords and Commons, assembled in Parliament at Westminster.

The Humble PETITION of the Knights, Gentry, Clergy, and Commonality of the County of KENT, *subscribed by the Grand Jury, on the 11th of May, 1648, at the Sessions of the Judges, upon a Special Commission of Oyer and Terminer, held at the Castle of Canterbury, for the said County.*

SHEWETH,

THAT the deep sense of our own miseries, with a fellow-feeling of the discontents of other Counties exposed to the like sufferings, prevaileth with us, thus humbly to present to your Honors these our ardent desires.

I. That our most Gracious Sovereign Lord KING CHARLES, may with all speed be admitted in safety and honor, to treat with his two Houses of Parliament, for the perfect settling of the peace, both of Church and Common Wealth, as also of his own just Rights, together with those of the Parliament.

II. That for prevention and removal of the manifold Inconveniencies, occasioned by the continuance of the present Army, under the command of the Lord Fairfax, their Arrears may be forthwith audited, and they disbanded.

III. That according to the fundamental Constitution of this Common Wealth, we may for the future be governed and judged by the English Subjects undoubted birth-right, the known and established Laws of the Kingdom, and not otherwise.

IV. That, according to the Petition of our Right, our Property may not be invaded by any Taxes or Impositions whatsoever; and particularly, that the heavy burthen of Excise may no longer be continued, or hereafter imposed upon us.

> All which our earnest desires, we humbly recommend to your serious considerations, not doubting of that speedy satisfaction therein which the case requires, and we humbly expect. Whereby we may hope to see (what otherwise we cannot but despair of) a speedy and happy end of those Pressures and Distempers, whose continuance will inevitably ruin both ourselves and posterities. Your timely prevention whereof, by a mutual agreement to what we here propose, in order thereunto, shall oblige us ever to pray.

Which Petition soon obtained the approbation of the Gentry and Clergy, excepting some who were troubled with the heart-burning faction, and could not digest so great a state pill. Some Deputy Lieutenants also approved of it, and directly signed it; several others seemed to be of the same opinion; but when they were to sign it, slipped their necks out of the collar, and left the city; but that day it was signed by above two hundred gentlemen then in the city; and copies transcribed and dispersed amongst them all; by which means, by a quick flight they were dispersed over all the county also; there being so many gentlemen then met together from every division and hundred, a more fitting opportunity could never have happened. Then on the backside of every Petition was endorsed this postscript.

"It is desired, that all copies and subscriptions be brought into Rochester, on Monday, the 29th of this instant May, 1648. And that all who intend to accompany this Petition, do meet at Black-Heath the day following, by nine of the clock in the morning."

By this means, the whole county might unanimously go, not only in their subscriptions, but in the presentation of it to the Parliament.

But there were at the same time some of the Grandees in the city, who by no means could swallow it, least it should have choked their reputation with the House; and indeed, being stung with too guilty a conscience, found this pill too harsh a corrosive to them.

Amongst the rest, Sir Henry Heyman, and Sir Michael Lusey, who posted immediately away to give them a timely notice, for prevention of a design so honorable, conscientious and religious, but absolutely destructive to their interest and proceedings; or at least, that they might, by being praemoniti, be also praemuniti, which two are seldom other than correlatives; the one drawing a usual consequence from the other, as indeed it proved by them; as will afterwards appear by their votes and stratagems against it.

But e'er they went, out of tender affection his rebellious bowels yearned with towards his brethren in iniquity, went to the prison where White the barber lay for his horrid villainy, (the man not being yet recovered) and brought him out, with hat in hand, giving him thanks for his good service and extraordinary zeal for the cause, and set him at liberty, without being questioned for the fact.

On the Sunday following, several letters were sent from the Speaker of the Lower House, to all the Deputy Lieutenants of the County, and what Justices of Peace the Members thought proper, that they knew an intended Petition was to be presented to the House from that County, desiring them to use their utmost endeavours for the effectual preventing of it, and suppressing the people in it.

Never disputing the justice of it, nor injustice of themselves in denying the proceeding of it; for, any man that knows how to judge between right and wrong almost in any thing, is certain, that the intentions of a King's calling a Parliament, are for the speedy redressing the grievances of his kingdom, and the admitting by him, and the choosing by the People, the Commons into Parliament, is for no other reason, than to represent the grievances of the Commons in general, for that part of the kingdom they served as representatives, by way of Petition, from them to the King and Lords for redress; but the Constitution of Parliament was so altered by their new-invented Kirk-

Laws of Reformation, that no man, no, not the best politicians are physicians good enough to feel its pulse, though in a most horrid distraction of ill humours; and our blessed Reformers had so long fought for the privilege of Parliament, that they had both lost that, and the liberty, and the true rights of the Subject, with the prerogative of the King to boot; and metamorphosed the Laws of the Kingdom into the shapeless monster of an arbitrary Government and tyrannous power of the sword.

But these letters also, they were authorised to seize, and surprise all persons they should find, or suspect to be instigators in the prosecution of it; and to secure all castles, towns and garrisons in the county; and by their greatest care, to prevent all public meetings at any places whatsoever within the county, except their own. Then began the Committee to noise abroad their ill menaces, with threatenings to all such as should dare to prosecute so horrid a villainy, and tumultuous seditions, as they termed it; and published a libellous order against it, and all such as should sign it, or any way forward the progress of it amongst the people, by any public or sinister means. The order was as follows.

By the Deputy Lieutenants of the County of Kent, the City and County of Canterbury, at their general meeting at Maidstone, on the 16th of May, 1648.

"WHEREAS we understand, that divers persons have given out, that they intend to assemble themselves towards the latter end of this month, or the beginning of the next, at several times, and in several places, on pretence of carrying a Petition to the Parliament, which doth relate to affairs against the authority of both Houses, and tendeth to the raising of seditions and tumults within this county. We have received a special command from the House of Commons, to use our best endeavours for the preserving of the peace of that county, do hereby, in order thereunto, advise all whom it may concern, to forbear all occasions of public disturbances, by any such pretence whatsoever; and if any well-affected persons, have been abused and misled, so as to sign, or procure hands to any such seditious paper, under the name of a Petition, and upon false giving out, that the Deputy Lieutenants of this County do approve thereof, to the end that such well-meaning persons may be undeceived, (we having seen a copy of the said Petition) do hereby signify our utter detestation of such seditious practices; and do advise all well-wishers to their country's peace, to take heed thereof, and to council and persuade their neighbours accordingly; and, if any pretended copies of such pretended Petition come unto, or be in their hands, to deliver the same unto the next Deputy Lieutenant."

"And we do hereby require the Ministers of the several parishes, publicly to read this Order and Signification in their parish churches, upon the next Lord's Day after the receipt hereof, immediately before they begin their morning sermon; and the Church-wardens of the several parishes, are hereby required, the next day after the time appointed for the publication, to certify what hath been done therein, under their hands unto the next Deputy Lieutenants, who are hereby directed forthwith to transmit the said Certificate to the standing Committee at Maidstone, so that notice may be taken what Ministers and Church-wardens do their duty therein; and such as shall be found negligent in the performance of this order, shall be proceeded against accordingly."

Anthony Wilding	*Thomas Syliard,*
John Rivers,	*Lambert Godfrey,*
Richard Lee,	*William James*
Thomas Lewis,	*John Bix,*
James Oxenden	*William Keniorash,*
Richard Beale,	

To the MAYOR of GRAVESEND, who is hereby required to cause proclamation hereof to be read in open market, next day after the receipt hereof, in the height of the market, by the common Cryer, and afterwards to deliver it to the Minister of the said parish to read it in the church.

But this violent course of theirs, in endeavouring to obstruct, added rather a vigorous life to it, and made it fly through the county with a far greater velocity, and the more exasperated the whole country to a prosecution of it, according to the saying of Seneca; *Patentia laesa fit furor.*

The whole country being by this means enraged, they resolved upon the prosecution of their Petition, being so far engaged, notwithstanding all obstructions whatever; which caused many meetings of the Gentry in Canterbury and Rochester, and divers other places of the county, at which meetings, the business was more deliberately weighed; and, upon serious consideration, found themselves likely to be lost in a maze of inconveniencies, if they went not resolutely forward in what they had begun. Whereupon this order of the Committee was reviewed, and a vindication of their proceedings in answer to it, drawn up and published.

An exact copy of the said Vindication followeth.

The Petitioner's Vindication and Answer to the Deputy Lieutenant's Declaration against the said Petition.

"WE the, Knights, Gentry, Clergy, and Commonality of the County of Kent, who have subscribed, and do intend to present the real Petition, (which is absolutely called a pretended one, and a seditious paper) to the Honorable the Lords and Commons assembled in Parliament at Westminster, according to the just rights and privileges of the subjects of England, in pursuance of the subscription of the Grand Jury of our county, on the 11th of May, 1648, (who are, and ought to be representers of the sense of our County) have taken notice of a late order or declaration of the Deputy Lieutenants of our county, of the 16th of May, 1648, tending to the discountenancing and suppressing of the said Petition; and untruly charging the same to contain matter against the authority of the Lords and Commons, to whom it is addressed; and the petitioners to be the raisers of sedition and tumults: in a deep sense whereof, and indignation of such false scandals imposed on us, we do declare to the world,

That the matter of the Petition, contains in it nothing but what is just, and fit for free-born subjects to demand, and tends to the preserving of the peace, not only of our county, but of the whole kingdom.

And the manner of our intentions to prosecute the same, shall be so peaceable on our parts, as shall not give occasion of tumults or public disturbances."

We do protest against raising of any factions against the Parliament, to whom we address ourselves for a just relief of our grievances; in pursuance of the right of subjects, and their own ordinances, and our intentions so peaceable, we must declare.

That, notwithstanding all menacing threats, published to our discouragement, we shall go on to prosecute our just rights and desires, in such a way as shall neither render us guilty of sedition or public disturbance; nor of betraying ourselves to the violence of such who shall endeavour unjustly to oppose us.

And we do desire all persons of our county, (well affected to the said Petition) not to be discouraged from the just prosecution thereof, on any threats or orders whatever: our intentions being, (if it shall please God to dispose us) to sacrifice our lives and fortunes in the prosecution of these our just rights and desires.

We have not a desire to deceive any man, nor have we endeavoured to mislead any, with pretending the Deputy Lieutenant's approbation of our Petition: nor do we desire any to join with us, but those, whose reason and conscience dictates to themselves the sense of our Petition."

Now the Committees began to bestir themselves on the other party with more resolution; because they saw threats would no way prevail to their advantage, and sent out their warrants for all the trained troops and companies to meet at rendezvous at several places in the county. But this would neither avail nor any way answer their expectation; for not any gave in answer to their warrants, but rather absented themselves from their habitations, except Captain Foach and some of his troops; who, with about twenty of his men met together, and marched away to Maidstone, there to attend the Committee, who thought by this time to consider of their own security. Sir T——T——sent out his warrants likewise, to meet at Barnham Downs, where appeared about ten, but not one officer, nor any colours, for his officers were all engaged in the prosecution of the Petition. He waited there near all the day, in constant hope and expectation of their coming; but towards night, no more appearing, he dispatched his man to Canterbury, to see if any were met together there, and to invite them, for he dare not command; but his Worship's man no sooner entered the gates of the city, but he was surprised by a guard there, and dismounted, and so forced to retire back to his master on foot. In the interim, Sir T—-staying on the Downs with the few men he had, was minded to drink, and calling for beer, one of his men drank the King's health to him, which relished not well with his palate, having a great while been a trusty friend for the Parliament; and, as he said, not being accustomed to drink health's, it would impair his health, but indeed was somewhat jealous they did it with a view of advancing some other inconveniency to him; whereupon, he stole away from them, and clapping his heels to his mule, (for spurs he seldom wore) away he rode, John like, never making any stop, till he thought he was out of danger of the cannon-jug, and like a hare regarded nothing before him; by chance, overtaking another of the Deputy Lieutenants, more leisurely moving along, and ruminating upon the business, he had certainly over-run him, had his beast been capable to have performed it, without taking any notice of him; so extraordinary was his haste, as I was informed by the said Deputy Lieutenant himself.

Now, it being high time, the gentlemen engaged in the Petition began to consider farther of their interest; and, being so strongly engaged how to make good what they had done, and which way with most security, to go forwards; for not to perfect what they had undertook, was not only to undo it, but themselves also without dispute; wherefore, they met constantly every day, considering withal, the eminent danger of that perpetual slavery, not only they, but the kingdom in general, was fallen into; and the extremity of violence, the grand taxation of the kingdom did threaten to crush them with; but instead of asking favour at their hands, (as the Children of Israel did, while under the cruel tyranny of Pharaoh) resolved, like Men of Kent, to maintain, if it were possible, their ancient rights and liberties, or to perish in the attempt, which they knew indeed would be a hard matter for them, having such an infection within themselves, and over the major part of the county; insomuch, that they knew not any found part in it; but that most of them were likely enough to cherish and breed up vermin to destroy it; but yet, notwithstanding their lofty menaces and bug-bear threats, to proceed in their engagements. Whereupon a Manifesto was drawn up by them, and signed as an absolute and unanimous engagement among themselves, and afterwards dispersed to the view of the whole world, that all might know the candid reality of their resolution.

THE MANIFESTO

"THAT the innocency of our intentions, and justice of our undertakings may clearly appear to all men of uncorrupt understandings, and hearts not too servile, by the long and odious custom of oppression, we, the Knights, Clergy, and Freeholders, of the county of Kent, (the most free people of this late flourishing nation, by the wisdom of our ancestors delivered from the Laws of the Conqueror, and to the late days of unhappy confusion and distraction, through all the reigns of the most glorious and victorious kings and princes of this nation) do hereby declare, and manifest to all the world, that our meetings and assembling together, is no other than a vindication of ourselves and purposes, from the scandal and aspersions of the Committee of this county; who, upon occasion of a Petition, in behalf of the county of Kent, assented and subscribed to, by the Grand Jury, at the Session of the Judges, upon special Commission of Oyer and Terminer, executed at the Castle of Canterbury, on the 11th of this instant May, for the said county, have not only made orders against the same, but commanded them to be read publicly in all churches, passing sentence and condemnation on the said Petition and all the Abettors; and have summoned the troops of horse, and forces of foot of this county, for suppression of the said Petition; which tends not only to the suppression of the liberty even of the most enslaved persons in the world; but also, as much as in them lies, show their endeavour, upon any cause whatever, which suit not with their temper, to over-rule the judgments of other persons; and meeting with opposition, think they have sufficient reason to destroy the lives and fortunes (or both) of their opposer's ."

"In consideration whereof, and that now the said Committee finding themselves unable to involve this county in blood, have made their addresses to the Parliament and Army; and make strange and malicious representations of our purposes, thereby discovering nothing so much as their own pride and malice.

We, the said Knights, Gentlemen, Clergy, and Free-Yeomen of the said county of Kent, do hereby appeal to all the world to judge, if it were not high time for us to put ourselves in a posture of defence? And do farther declare, that we will prosecute our said Petition, with our lives and fortunes, not doubting of a fair reception from both Houses of Parliament, whom we know to have been instigated against us by the said Committee.

And therefore, saving to ourselves the enlarging the said Petition, we have resolved to charge the said Committee with increasing the taxes of this county above due proportion, only for maintaining their own private luxury and pride; with usurping a power over the estates and fortunes of the freemen of this county, not granted to them by any power of Parliament; and with a tyrannical, unlimited and embittered spirit naturally engrafted in them, and expressed by words and actions during the exercise of this power, (which makes them unfit to rule) to the exasperating the peoples' hearts into all animosities, and overthrowing of all love and peace in this county; which also hath been followed to that height of persecution, that had not the Lords and Commons put a stop to their exorbitant proceedings, we had suffered much more under the torment of "these men's projected designs."

And we do hereby acknowledge ourselves to have been secured in the temper and moderation of the Parliament. We have no more to say or do, but to defend ourselves till we can have a right understanding of our purposes and actions before the Parliament. In the mean time, we shall look on all opposition as the provocation of a conscious and endangered Committee; and in respect to the invasion lately made upon the persons of our neighbours, we think it not proper to lie at the mercy of the soldiers, but have recourse to arms, from which, no threatenings or fear of the army shall drive us away, knowing well the justice of our cause, and the temper of our hearts."

Thus they resolved to proceed in their design, seizing all the arms and ammunition at Scot's-Hall, Ashford, Feversham, &c. whilst Sir Michael Lusey and others of the Deputy Lieutenants seemed to act to the utmost of their power, for the suppressing of them; but—Hales, Esq. a man well esteemed for his honor and integrity, in a short time had raised a great party, in that part of the county, and falling to work with those bold opposers, soon destroyed their power, and laid their honor in the dust, till at last they were forced to seek a better security than their arms; and took sanctuary in Sir Peter Ricot's house at Ailsford but the foxes lay not long there, before the terriers were so near forcing them forth, that they were glad to make conditions for leave to run away; which being granted, they delivered up the house, a great magazine of arms and ammunition, which proved very serviceable to the victors.

In the interim, other parties being increased and formed in order, kept moving up and down, and received all who wished well, and had signed and engaged in the Petition, who were so unanimous, that within two day's space, there were strong parties of them got together near Wye, Ashford, Rochester and Gravesend, and several other places; insomuch, that all the Committee were glad to make trial of the old proverb, "One pair of legs "is worth two pair of hands," so posted to London to tell a lamentable story to the Parliament.

Captain Lee and another Member of Parliament, were sent down by order of the House, and came to Rochester, to parley with those that were met there; where, upon debate of the business, they used the greatest policy to persuade them to accept of an act of indemnity from the Parliament, and lay aside their designs; but these gentlemen were immediately confined, and forced to treat for their own indemnity at last; for well the engagers knew what the indemnity of the Parliament would be, if once they laid their swords out of their hands, and submitted to the mercy of theirs.

On Tuesday, the 23rd of May, a great number of knights and gentlemen met at Canterbury, intending one and the same interest, being active and vigorous in advancing the affair in hand, not minding any other concern, than the public welfare; concluding with a magnanimous courage, to march with the Petition in one hand and a Sword in the other; though not as some had falsely and maliciously asserted, to force the higher powers to what they should fancy or desire, which they might have done according to the examples of that kind, showed by those they had to deal with, the law being now swallowed up into the unlimited arbitration and power of a blood-thirsty sword; but that they might thereby make way through all obstructions, and have liberty (according to the ancient custom of this realm) to represent their grievances to both Houses of Parliament, a thing which had never before been opposed, nor accounted riotous, till this Parliament, by their all-powerful arbitration voted it so.

This being a general resolution through the county, all men cheerfully took up arms; the commonality and inferior sort, submitting to the commands of their superiors, who, as commissioners, acted what by a general council was thought most convenient for the security of so great an engagement as they were now brought to: and that a clear and candid satisfaction for their arming themselves as aforesaid might be given to the whole kingdom, as well enemies as friends, caused the following Remonstrance to be published, having first been informed of the bloody answer their neighbours of Surrey had received to their peaceable and legal Petition, and for which inhuman massacre the butchering myrmidons had the thanks of the Parliament.

A

LETTER

FROM

Sʳ *MARMADVKE LANGDALE,*

Gᴇɴᴇʀᴀʟʟ of the *Northerne Forces;*

ᴛᴏ

Sir *CHARLES LVCAS:*

CONTAINING

A cleare *Relation* of all their *proceedings* in the *North* : VVith an hopefull aſſurance of a ſpeedy *Relief* to Cᴏʟᴄʜᴇsᴛᴇʀ.

After the Originall Copy, truly tranſcribed.

L O N D O N.
Printed in the Yeare, 1648.

THE REMONSTRANCE

"**B**EING reduced to this choice, either to deliver up our lives and liberties together, or die free; we are resolved to act the last scene of this tragedy, with our swords in our hands, which we shall sooner turn upon our own hearts than the public peace. By what necessities exasperated to this resolve, let the world determine, and understand, that our Petition to the religious and honorable Houses of Parliament, hath been opposed; and the petitioners menaced and persecuted into this extremity, by spirits most implacably distempered; in particular Sir Anthony Wilding, vowed he would not cross the street of Rochester, to save from ruin one soul who subscribed to the Petition: it was also the proposition of Mr. Beales, to hang two of the petitioners in every parish. If this be not enough to awaken others, let it suffice that it hath brought us to a just sense and scorn of those indignities: we have lost all with patience, and if at last it be accounted a crime to beg, we shall choose to perish. We do therefore solemnly and religiously oblige ourselves, with our lives and fortunes, to oppose effectually, those persons who shall presume to interrupt us in the just and legal presentation of our humble desires to both Houses of Parliament; and to the utmost of our endeavours to save the harmless, and protect each other in a privilege so undoubtedly our own; and which hath not only been adjudged such by this present Parliament, but practiced and encouraged by them. And further, in case any single person shall be prosecuted for this engagement, all of us to rise and rescue him. So help us God, as we shall respectively and resolutely perform."

Thus gallantly resolved were the greatest part of the gentry in the county of Kent; which behaviour encouraged also the commonality in as resolute a bravery and boldness: and indeed, it was high time to declare themselves, as the state of the kingdom threatened a dismal cloud of dull and sordid slavery, for the tyrants' swords had a long time drank the blood of the loyal-hearted gentry of this kingdom, and they were really insensible how they went on, or upon whom they exercised their cruelty.

On Tuesday about noon, the knights and gentlemen who where entrusted as commissioners at Canterbury, gave commission to Colonel Robert Hammon, to raise a regiment of foot by beat of drum, and Colonel Hatton for enlisting and raising a regiment of horse. Their commissions ran thus:

17

"For the more safe and speedy expedition in preferring the general Petition of this county, we, the Gentry, now interested and trusted herein, do nominate and appoint you, Robert Hammon, Colonel of one regiment of foot, &c."

Having the day before seized on the magazine of that part of the county then in Canterbury, containing a large quantity of arms and ammunition of all sorts; Colonel Hammon immediately beating up his drums, had in a short time enlisted a considerable number of men; more I think, than ever were enlisted by one man in so short a time.

Then Colonel Hatton, and Colonel Hammon, had orders to rendezvous the next day at Barnham Downs, where all the trained soldiers of that part of the county were appointed (by warrant of the Commissioners) to meet; but this day proving extraordinary wet, very much hindered their appearance.

However, Colonel Hammon with about three hundred foot, well accoutered and armed, and Colonel Hatton with about sixty horse: a good collection for so short a time as half a day to raise them in; but there came not in above two hundred trained men, by reason of the badness of the weather. Most of the Knights and Deputy Lieutenants in that part of the county also met here, for now many of the Deputy Lieutenants had joined with the Petitioners, although, I suppose, out of a politic consideration, not a cordial affection, as indeed did afterwards appear. There, after some consultations, they transacted many affairs for the advancement of the engagement, using their utmost endeavours for the raising not only of men, but money also, for the supporting and encouraging those who were not able to go through it themselves, being removed from all their callings and employments; engaging for the constant paying both of soldiers and officers, whilst they should continue in the service of their country; for the better advancement whereof, every gentleman according to his ability, subscribed to the loan of monies, some a hundred pounds, some eighty, some fifty, some forty, some more, and some less; and sent abroad their warrants into all parts of the county, for the summoning all such men as had, and would engage in that service, for the advancing the general safety of the county, and liberty of the kingdom.

Towards night, the rendezvous breaking up, Colonel Hammon and Colonel Hatton, marched off to quarter towards Dover; then Sir Richard Hardres, Sir Anthony Aucher, and Mr. Anthony Hammond, Justices of the Peace, and men as hearty, as real, and as indulgently industrious in the propagation of the engagement, as men could be; and Mr. Thomas Peak, with about seven score trained men, being then by reason of the wetness of the weather on horseback, as dragoons, marched towards Sandwich, having dispatched a messenger with a letter to the Mayor of the town before, to acquaint him of their coming, and intentions.

Upon their arrival there, they found the ports all shut, and guarded round about the town; then Mr. Matthew Carter, by appointment of the rest of the gentlemen, marching in the head of the men, gave a summons to them, but they at first refused to open the gates, till, after some parley with them, an officer asked him, whether Sir Richard Hardres was there or not, who was one of the Deputy Lieutenants for the Parliament, who coming to them, and demanding entrance, the Recorder of the town came out, and told him, that the Mayor's orders were, "That if he came, the gates should be opened, but not else;" so immediately they were, and marching quietly in, they drew up in the market-place, and first changed all the guards about the town, before they engaged in any other business, it being then almost night; then the Commissioners being together, they sent for the Mayor of the town, and demanding his subscription to the Petition, gave him orders for the raising of monies immediately, for the forwarding the affair; but he proved very slow in that service, pretending, that the town was very poor, and could by no means raise any; the Excise Officers were also called in, but their stores proved very poor also; insomuch, that there remained little hopes of any good to proceed from that place.

In the evening, came in a gentleman who had formerly been a divine, and a captain at sea, and was now a major in the service of the Parliament; he appeared then very penitent for having engaged himself in so unjust a cause and horrid engagement, and proffered the best and utmost of his service to the furthering the Petition and engagement of the county, if he might be employed in anything that might give him an opportunity; whereupon, they knowing him to have been at sea, and well acquainted with the navy, being both chaplain there to the Earl of Warwick, and minister of Deal, thought it could not prove amiss to employ him, having signed to the Petition before; and so had letters drawn up for him that night, to every ship one, and in every letter a copy of the Petition, making this absolute result, that some happy success might follow; however, if it did no good, yet it could no way detriment them; which indeed proved a most happy and fortunate design, as all the kingdom are witnesses of.

The next morning, being Thursday, the Mayor and Aldermen were again called upon, to know what monies they had raised, or would advance to that service, being solely for the re-enthronement of the King, (as they told them) and the speedy redemption of the most turkishly enslaved subjects of England, to their true, ancient, and native liberty; but they were then found as tardy as before; dull, and unwilling to endeavour, pleading the great necessity and inability of the town, as nothing touched with any consideration of loyalty or conscience, to their imprisoned King, or the bleeding distresses of their enslaved country; whereupon, the Commissioners did not think it either safe or convenient to entrust themselves with a military power; but took away the commissions from the Mayor, (who was captain of a trained company in the town) and the other trained captains, and disposed of the companies to other gentlemen in the town, such as for their honesty and loyalty, were thought worthy the trust. Then they cut to pieces the commission of the Captain of the auxiliary company; seized on the magazine of the town, loaded a wagon with powder, match and ball, for the present undertaking, and made all things ready for a march towards Dover.

But e'er they marched, the soldiers being again drawn up to their colours in the market-place, the Commissioners went to pay a visit to a stripling impostor, who lodged (by order of the Mayor and his wise brethren) at Captain Forstall's house, one of the jurat's who pretended to be the Prince of Wales, and that he was forced to leave France, for the Queen (his mother) had endeavoured to poison him; which notable project he had seriously insinuated into the general opinions, both of town and country, by his often affirming it with impudent oaths and horrid expressions; insomuch, that many gentlemen and ladies came daily to kiss his hand, and many fine presents they made him: rich cloaths and accommodation was provided for him, by the Mayor and Jurates of the town, who were so serious in it, that Sir Thomas Dishingto, a Scotchman, being upon a message from the Queen and Prince into England, and coming to Dover, in his way back again, hearing it generally reported in the county, of the Prince's being at Sandwich, was very much surprised, and to satisfy himself, went to Sandwich to be informed; when he found him a Welsh Prince indeed, but not the Prince of Wales; and coming to him, after some discourse, asked him who was his Gentleman-Usher? where the Queen was when he left her? and the like questions: he not being well provided with answers, every person present was convinced of his being an impostor; and Sir Thomas Dishingto did thereupon call him villain, counterfeit rogue, &c. which language offending the new-coined Prince, he commanded the Mayor to commit him to prison for treason: the Mayor obeyed his command, and Sir Thomas, instead of continuing his journey to Dover, was hurried away to goal, where he lay two days before he was set at liberty.

The Sunday after Sir Thomas's commitment, Mr. Carter went to see the sham Prince, in order, not only to satisfy himself in the truth of the affair, but also certain Deputy Lieutenants in the county. He was lodged at Captain Forstall's house, whither he came on foot, dressed in an old black suit, having no companions but lice; and on seeing him, Mr. Carter assured Captain Forstall and others, that he was an impostor; but they would not be convinced of the folly of their confidence, and the youth carried on the cheat upwards of a week, having a guard of musqueteers to attend him, trumpets sounding whilst at meat, and most nights went drunk to bed.

The Commissioners having received an exact account of his behaviour, (and finding the hearts of the people were much inclined to him, as believing what he said to be true) were minded to carry him away with them, imagining he was sent into the county upon an ill design, by some who had long enjoyed a power of marring princes, though not of making any; and accordingly, early one morning they went to his lodgings, having an empty coach of Sir Richard Hardres's, in which they intended to convey him, and offered to free him from the restraint which he pretended to lie under, by a declaration he had published; fearing, that if they took him away in a forcible manner, it might occasion a disturbance in the town and country; but this design would not take, for on their appearance before the house, the pretended Prince and his confederates refused to admit them, and Captain Forstall shut up his doors, telling them that the Prince had commanded him to keep them out, and he dare not disobey him.

At which refusal the Commissioners being highly affronted, desired Mr. Carter to draw up sixty musqueteers before the house and force an entrance, which party Mr. Carter drew up immediately, and they stood to their arms, loaded their musquets, and lighted their matches, expecting to be suddenly employed; and now the whole town appeared in a mutinous and distracted condition; insomuch that the Commissioners themselves were forced to prepare for battle, and an engagement being momentarily expected, all houses and shops were commanded to be shut up. In the mean time the young Impostor, triumphing in his new-invested authority, waved his hat and plume out at the window, crying, Raise the town! Raise the town! Seamen, stand to me, Seamen! at the same time throwing handfuls of money among the people in the street, who swarmed up and down in throngs and tumults. The women wept for fear their Prince should be misused; the men swore they would all die rather than suffer the Prince to be any way injured, or forcibly taken away; some really believing him to be the Prince of Wales, others were confederates in his design. The tumult must have ended in much mischief, had not the gentlemen resolutely and undauntedly bestirr'd themselves in quelling the disorder.

Whilst they were forcing an entrance into the house, the confederates within privately conveyed him out at the back door, where he was received by the seamen, who hurried him on board a vessel, and transported him to the Isle of Thanet; but a party being sent after him, found him that night at supper with Mr. Crisp, who was entertaining him as elegantly as if he had been the real Prince of Wales. He was taken into custody, and conducted to Canterbury, in Mr. Crisp's coach, and afterwards committed to Newgate.

They also took up Captain Forstall, and charged him with being a confident in the designs of the mock Prince, by refusing them admittance, and thereby occasioned the disorder in the town; and would have committed him, had he not positively affirmed, that he really believed him to be the Prince, and that what he did was by his command, and that he was afraid to disobey him; then the Town Clerk engaging for his appearance when called upon to answer for his misbehaviour, he was released.

The gentlemen then left some of the men whom they brought with them, and an officer in the said town, for the security thereof, and ordering the new captains to summons their companies to arms, they marched away with the remainder for Dover.

At Dover they met Colonel Hammon's regiment, which was then increased to upwards of five hundred; and Colonel Hatton's of horse to about two hundred; who pursuant to their orders were drawing up to face the castle, with some trained companies of that part of the county; having several carts with scaling-ladders, spades, shovels and pick-axes.

They were received by the town with much joy and alacrity; Captain Bethel's fort resigned to them, and the town unanimously betook themselves to arms;

the trained men (being two companies) also joined them in this promising design.

In the afternoon, divers summons were sent to the castle, demanding the surrender of it for the service of the King and Country, but all denied.

Sir Henry H——, a grand independent and parliament man, being in the castle, bore great sway, and was their chief commander, though in reality had no power for acting; by whose order they had made incursions upon the country people a night or two before, and drove many sheep into the castle, as if every one was at liberty to act according to his own mind, for promoting the general calamity of the kingdom; no matter at what expense to others, so their own interest was secure. So large an extent had their arbitrary prerogative and unlimited illegal jurisdiction, that they abhorred, as destructive, the dictates of their conscience, or thoughts of affection to the peace of their country; this plainly appeared by the answers Sir Henry returned to the letters and propositions which were sent from the Commissioners to him whilst in the castle; as if the burthen of intolerable guilt of innocent blood, and unparalleled misery of this gasping nation, had overwhelmed his conscience with a cloud of despair of any other safety than the old Roman rule; *Per scelera semper, sceleribus tutum est iter*; well knowing himself to have been as zealous a promoter and accessory in the general calamity, as any person whatsoever; and to whom the name of peace was as odious, as the thoughts of the punishment which he knew he justly deserved, and if given up to justice, and tried by the laws of the kingdom, must unavoidably have perished; for though his resolution was like Cataline's, yet his end must be as the Tyrants of Athen's, whose proceedings he imitated.

They again sent a summons to the castle, and a civil letter to Sir Henry H—, inviting him to surrender, or at least to desist from his engagement, promising him a secure retreat to any part of the county, or to London, if he was minded to go thither, or elsewhere; but he refused to hearken to any of those offers; and by his means, with the assistance of Lieutenant Swan, the people in the castle were kept from a surrender, though most of them were willing so to do.

The above-named Lieutenant Swan, had some time before received a commission from the Prince, engaging his faith to act according to the same, but he only betrayed it, but endeavoured to take away the lives of several gentlemen concerned with him.

This night, Major Keme, who was dispatched on board the fleet returned, and assured the Commissioners, that the letters he carried, were received with great cheerfulness; that they were no sooner read, but the mariners, one and all, declared for the King, the liberties of the kingdom, and the engagement of the Gentlemen of Kent; boldly disputing the affair upon deck with arms in their hands, seeming fully resolved to do their utmost against those who should oppose them; and some officers and a few of the mariners, showing a dislike to their proceedings on board particular ships, though too weak to engage them, they were seized and confined in the holds of the ships they belonged to.

This being done, they made loud shouts and huzzas, which reached the ears of Colonel Rainsborow, then vice-admiral, who was on shore and upon the leads of the castle, flourishing his sword over his head with an air of defiance, whilst the Commissioners and Gentlemen marched by; and being surprised at the acclamations aforesaid, and finding they did not proceed from one ship only, but from every one then riding at anchor in the Downs, hasted away, designing to go on board; but on his coming near the Admiral's ship, the mariners forced the boat off, telling him, "He had nothing to do with them, nor should he." He demanded to know the reason of this sudden and amazing alteration? They immediately answered,
"They were upon different designs than those they knew he would lead them upon, or join with them in, having declared themselves for the King and the Gentlemen of Kent."
At the same time acknowledging, that he had been a kind and good-natured commander to them, in return for which, no injury should be done him, nor should he suffer the least damage in person or goods, and the effects belonging to him, then on board the ship, should be safely delivered on demand.

The Colonel seeing them so serious and resolute, demanded a pinnace to carry him to London, being fearful of turning himself on shore, though he had the command of Deal castle given him in his commission; upon which, a Coxon stepping upon deck, answered him in these words:
"Sir, we cannot spare you the least vessel in the Downs; they are engaged for better service: There is a Dutch fly-boat on shore, and for sixpence, you may have a passage in her to London:" This answer much confused him, and increased his apprehension of danger, insomuch that he thought himself unsafe

both at sea and on shore, having received advice that Sandown castle had joined with the Navy, and declared for the King and Country; and expecting several others to follow their example, he took the Coxon's advice, and taking on board his wife, children, sisters, and the rest of his family, then in Deal castle, made the greatest haste to London, and gave his masters an exact account of his honorable escape.

Major Keme having finished the account of his good success, was dispatched away with letters of summons to the other two castles of Deal and Wamer, having also instructions and power to treat with them for surrender; which actions, though they carried a martial face with them at that time, in the opinion of our enemies, yet were done in the most prudent and cautious manner; for who could but think it very unsafe for that part of the country, and dangerous both to public and private interest, to leave the strongest holds in the possession of a violent and bloody enemy, to make incursions upon the inhabitants when they pleased, the chief strength of the county being to march away with the Petition; the ill consequence of which, the defenders of Dover castle had given us a convincing proof of a few nights before, when they sallied out, and plundered the country (especially those who were disaffected to the Parliament) and did much mischief.

But tis' not unworthy of remark, and that in all those proceedings, viz. in gaining over the fleet, and taking possession of the towns, not the least prejudice or damage was done to any man, either in person, estate, or goods. Then were letters sent into France, and Holland, with engagement of the gentry and merchants, for the bringing over ten thousand arms, and a great quantity of ammunition of all sorts; as letters also to the Prince, to give him an account of all proceedings and intents of the engagers; altogether as honest, and as yet (by God's providence) so prosperous, that the gates of fortune seemed to be wide set open to their honorable resolutions, being nothing intended, or inclinable to the raising of any offensive war, but the purchasing (though at the hazard of our lives and fortunes) of a happy and lasting peace; and that not in particular to ourselves, but generally to the Sion of our church and common wealth; for which, I think ought both to pray and fight, if rightly and loyally called to it.

And now having thus far proceeded, and with such auspicious success, they went on, and prosecuted their business with expedition, alacrity and courage, knowing the time admits of no delays, were danger is knocking at the door; that sloth and negligence in desperate and difficult enterprises, are the only advancements to ruin and destruction; but in extremities, and gaining of time is the purchase both of life and honorable success.

Therefore the next morning they marched from thence towards Deal castle, leaving in Dover, and before the castle, the trained bands of the town, and three other companies of that part of the country that were not gathered together, Mr. Arnold Brumes, and one or two more Justices of the Peace, and Commissioners for the County, were left to steer at the helm, lest for want of good pilots the undertaking should be wrecked. They drew up the great pieces which were planted on the beach, and mounted them on the most advantageous ground upon the hill near the castle; this they did with the loss of one man only, though both small and great shot were all the while played upon them very thick from the caste. The cannon being thus planted, on a very high hill, and but a small distance from the castle, they fired very briskly upon it and battered down the old walls very much; notwithstanding which, they refused to deliver it up, and storm it they could not.

The Commissioners with the rest of the gentlemen (which were a handsome company) marched on towards Deal, carrying with them Colonel Hammon's regiment, being by this time completed to a thousand, well armed, and as perfectly resolved, with colours flying, of white, answerable to the candid innocency of a peace-making engagement; and Colonel Hatton's horse, with some dragoons; the gentlemen, being about forty, were orderly drawn up in a troop, and marching all the way upon the Downs, made a handsome appearance both to the country on one side, and the ships riding at anchor in the Downs on the other, which gave encouragement to both, and also a disheartening to the castles, then on treaty for surrender.

The defenders of the castles discovering so orderly a body of men advancing towards them, sent to the Commissioners to desire that they would not draw any nearer, till they had concluded their conditions, the articles being then drawing up; whereupon a hault was made, and a rendezvous, the party also drawn up, and planted in orderly front towards the castles.

The Knights and Gentlemen then leaving them at the rendezvous, rode away to Deal, where the first (as indeed most requisite) thing they did, was the taking care for sending provisions to that small army they left in the field; and afterwards went on board the ships to take possession of them, and to place such officers as they thought fit to entrust with their command. Where they were received with great acclamations and expressions of joy.

There one might have read in every man's face a part of cheerfulness, as having been a long time like galley-slaves, chained to a more slavish condemnation than those in Turkey, and now happily set free into the glorious liberty of loyal obedience; and they expressed themselves so highly devoted to the service of the King and Country, that they would not only be commanded by sea, but desired they might have first admittance to be lifted ashore; but that would not be granted them by the Commissioners, for they would thereby have disfurnished their ships, and did not perceive they should have any need of them for land service; for now they thought, that although they expected nothing less than affronts and opposition, before they could perform what they had undertaken concerning the Petition; yet they supposed the county would unanimously join, and then there would be little want of number, able to force through all obstruction whatever. The foot party came in abundance at this time from all parts, and this happy success and gallant deportment of the gentry being a great encouragement to call them to their assistance, gave new life and courage to the commonality, and made them content on all occasions to join in that christian-like and loyal design. Although there were yet too many that lay lurking in their own habitations, to join with any enemy that should endeavour to make a prey of them, and help forward, upon any opportunity, so desperate a ruin; as if they cared not, though it turned to a general dissolution of the whole kingdom, and a most wretched and untimely fall to their too-indulgent, gloriously-virtuous, and unparallel'd patient sovereign; so that their own factious interest might recover its desired, but ignorantly-purposed end.

A nest of other cockatrices lay brooding also, as idly in the very heart of the country; nay, too many all over, whose dirty souls were so settled on the dregs of worldly interest, as depressed them down to so ignoble and cold a decision, that would not suffer them to look up to loyal obedience, nor permit their capacities to climb so high as a knowledge of that duty they owed to their King and Country; though their own interest was as much included as any that was the most active, every man being alike concerned in a general peace; and I think, according to his quality and condition, ought to endeavour as industriously for its advancement; many of them knew this too, yet so worldly-minded as to prefer the enjoyment of their estates, though like Jews under the worst of bondage, than like Christians, to hazard the impairing them only for the settled and assured enjoyment of them in the happiest liberty, the golden age of a just and religious peace, would give them for the future.

There were some Deputy Lieutenants also came in (for their security more than their conscience sakes, which they slubbered over with a counterfeit disguise of dissimulation, to purchase a better welcome) whom I could name too, but shall forbear; who coming in, and entering the lists with the loyal engagers, after they had not only signed the Petition, but warrants and commissions too, made a fair retreat, and bid farewell to the danger of proving loyal subjects, slipt their engaged collar, and stole away to London, and justly deserved a halter for it hereafter, as well as the rest of the greatest opposers; but I suppose before this, though not in respect of their fortunes, for which they may rejoice, yet in respect to the better wealth of their souls, they may have undergone so much of repentance, as may purchase a pardon from heaven, which my charity makes me hope, rather than with the contrary; and they were sensible enough they had a Sovereign to deal with, so far inheritor of his Father's virtues, as well as honors and prerogative, as by his excess of mercy, to mitigate the rigor of treason and law against them.

But to return to our new Sea-Royalists, who not only thought, but expressed also the great happiness of their changed condition; many of them saying cheerfully, "They now only lived, having a long time, as it were, lain amazed betwixt life and death, and desired rather to die in the service of their King, than to live again in that of the Parliament."

All which the Commissioners were overjoyed to see, and encouraged them in their gallant loyalty, giving amongst them in every ship, a sum of money to drink, which they gratefully received; and at their putting off to shore, gave them from every vessel many shot, answered with as many shouts and acclamations; but many of the mariners were so eager in prosecuting this new-engaged loyalty, that the greatest difficulty in managing them, proved in the keeping them aboard, being almost mutinous to come ashore, to list themselves for land service, as believing they should not find any opposition at sea, or at least, not time enough for them to express in their actions, what they had already done in their words, and as absolutely resolved in their hearts, as was the expression of many of them.

Which, to make up the more complete, they afterwards of themselves sent away a messenger to the Commissioners of the Navy, with this declaration following.

The Declaration of the Navy, in a Letter to the Commissioners at London.

Worshipful,

THESE are to certify you, that we the Commanders and Officers of the ship, called the Constant Reformation, with the rest of the fleet, have secured the ships for the service of the King and Parliament; and we have refused to be under the command of Colonel Rainsborow, by reason we conceive him to be a man not well affected to the King; and we do hereby declare unto you, that we have unanimously joined with the Kentish Gentlemen in their just Petition to the Parliament, to this purpose following, viz.

I. That the King's Majesty may be with all expedition admitted in safety, honor and freedom, to treat with his two Houses of Parliament.

II. That the Army now under the command of the Lord Fairfax, their arrears being paid them, be forthwith disbanded.

III. "That the known Laws of the Kingdom may be re-established and continued, whereby we ought to be governed and judged.

IV. That the privileges of Parliament, and the liberty of the subjects may be preserved. And to this end and purpose, we have sent our loving friend, Captain Penrose, with a letter to the Earl of Warwick; and we are resolved to take in no commander whatsoever, but such as shall resolve to live and die with us, in behalf of the Kingdom and Parliament, which is the positive result of us. And we humbly desire your speedy answer."

OFFICERS OF THE CONSTANT REFORMATION.

Thomas Lisle, Lieutenant,
Andrew Michell, Boatswain,
James Allen, Gunner,
Thomas Best, Carpenter.

OFFICERS OF THE SWALLOW.

Leonard Harris, Captain,
John London, Master,
Nicholas Lawrance, Lieutenant,
Andrew Jackson, Gunner,
John Short, Carpenter.

Signed also by the Captain of the Roebuck, *Hynde,* and
several other Officers of these and other ships.

This evening, the articles for the castles of Deal and Wamer were signed; and the one delivered before, the other after the Commissioners marched away. Their conditions upon surrender, were to march away with their baggage, leaving their arms and ammunition behind them entirely, without any embezzlement or diminution.

The rendezvous being broke up, they marched away and quartered in Sandwich, again that night, leaving in Deal, Anthony Hammond, Esq. and Captain Bargrave, who had been formerly an officer in the Navy; both justices of the peace, and gallant discreet men, (not according to those of this wise reformation) as Commissioners for managing the business there, and in the fleet; having sent away for Sir John Mince, Captain Fogg, and some other officers that had formerly served the King at sea, and for their loyalty, displaced by the Parliament, who were also earnestly desired by the officers and mariners aboard.

When they came to Sandwich, having been so prosperous in all these undertakings, and done so much in so little time, as indeed amazed the whole country, the Mayor and his brethren began to comply, and received them with far more cheerfulness than they had done before; and that night made them a present of two hundred pounds, to the advancement of the design, who before were so needy that they knew not how to subsist among themselves, much less to raise any sum of money for extraordinary service.

The next morning they hasted their march from thence to Canterbury, leaving only behind them two or three Commissioners, and five trained companies, for the better securing that town, being a place very factious, and apt to take the opportunity of the weakness of the country, to make a mutinous opposition in case of a retreat.

That night (being Sunday) they quartered in Canterbury, not missing any opportunity or minute of time, without an improvement of it to the best advantage, and acting something to the furtherance of their engagement, the next day being the appointed limitation for their meeting at Rochester. Here, there came in many gentlemen and others to join with them, that were not at all engaged before, unless against us; among the rest, was Sir John Roberts, and one or two Deputy Lieutenants more, who had signed the Petition, and subscribed to the loan of money, although they had before engaged themselves with the rest of the Committee against the Petition; but rather like Physicians, who out of a private interest, are ready to assist than out of any inward affection, to so just and honest an enterprise.

The Dutchmen of the city (which indeed were very numerous) engaged themselves for the raising and paying of two companies; here Colonel Hammon completed his regiment also, many more men joining him; and others that he had raised in the city, they were almost in readiness for a further march.

In this city and suburbs were three trained companies, which were also drawn up to arms, and that they might secure the place with two Dutch companies then raising, they left behind them some knights and gentlemen to manage affairs in that part of the county, least an insurrection should happen by the obstructers of the design, who gathered about the place, and by surprising it, might do great mischief in the rear of the body, in case of a retreat, which unfortunately happened in the end, provision for which ought at all times to be made in the strongest and most prosperous armies.

At this time, the Earl of Thanet, a noble peer, acted a very mean part; he was the first that rose in that part of the country, and drew the people about Ashford, Hatfield and Charing, to a resolution of taking up arms; he also sent letters to the gentlemen who had any interest or power thereabouts, and secured above a thousand men, who were ready to rise on the shortest notice; in particular James Hales, Esq. joined him, and behaved in a gallant manner.

Thus, after the said Earl had made a fair and promising beginning, and given large assurances of assistance from his purse, he went back from this scene of honor, and obscured himself behind the hangings of apostatism: insomuch, that when he was sought for by the neighbouring gentlemen, whom he had enticed by his forwardness, and invited by his persuasions, the noble Earl was said (not for religion) to consult with the Earl of Pembroke; who, after some discourse, prevailed upon him to go with him to Derby-House, where he pleaded for forgiveness, promising if he might but escape a whipping, never to do so again.

At the same time, this Earl made what discovery he could of the whole action: also, made several propositions to the Committee, which he assured them was the only way to remove those grievances complained of; declaring, that what he had proposed, he had heard from divers gentlemen in the engagement.

Whereupon the Committee began to hearken a little to his discourse, and gave some credit to it, having his friend and cousin Pembroke to swear for him; and thereupon resolved some instructions should be given him concerning indemnity, upon a submission again to the yoke, and the like conditions; which being reported to the House, were resolved on, and on the Thursday morning he was dispatched away with them.

Upon his coming home, with his greatest power, endeavoured the disbanding of the commonality; beginning first with the discouraging the gentry, who being once down, the other must necessarily fall; and indeed proceeded so far in it, that he caused divers gentlemen, as well as commoners, to desert the business; but the generality being constant, and their consciences linked to the service, by the golden chain of religion and loyalty, were not to be disheartened; insomuch, that those stratagems and endeavours for suppression, gave a more courageous life to their actions, and converted that pestiferous obstruction to a cordial advancement.

The gentlemen and commoners were not only sensible of his baseness, but were also incensed at it, and gave the Earl the following letter to deliver up to the Committee.

To the right honorable the Committee of the Lords and Commons at Derby House.

My Lords,

"We have seen the instructions from your Lordships, to the right honorable the Earl of Thanet, upon consideration whereof, we have thought fit to return this answer to your Lordships:

That we have cause to believe there are many persons about your Lordships, who endeavour to infuse into you sinister opinions of our proceedings, in relation to the safety of the county at this time; who, when we shall be admitted to a fair and equal hearing, will appear to be the greatest disturbers thereof themselves. And that our intentions are free from all other ends than natural defence. We humbly beseech your Lordships to understand, that we are in firm resolutions to observe the declaration of the Houses, and for the manner of presenting our Petitions and complaints, will follow the directions of the said declaration; but saving to ourselves always the liberty of preserving the most ancient and inviolate freedoms of this county, we must desire your Lordships to put a fair interpretation upon our purposes of continuing within the safeguard of our arms, till we have assurance from your Lordships, that the clamors of those above against us, have had no success in their enraged designs of engaging against this country in blood and ruin, when they find never so small a diminution of arbitrary power, so long exercised over us, endeavoured to be taken from them; not doubting, but upon presentation and fair reception of our Petition and just complaints, the Parliament will give such reasonable relief therein, as will abundantly discover the inclination of this county to peace and amity.

My Lords, this is the account we can give you of this county, by the hands of the noble Lord, the Earl of Thanet, whom also we have desired to inform your Lordships farther; that our present posture tends not to offer violence to the Parliament, nor suffer acts willingly, unbecoming our fair intentions; but we shall take strict care to repress wheresoever we find it, the incensed spirit we see in the people, which how it hath been raised, we shall in due time be able to make appear;   And we rest,

My Lords,
Your Lordship's
Most humble servants,

Thomas Peyton, Edward Whitton, John Darell, William Hugesson, Thomas Palmer, Richard Lee, jun. James Hales, James Darell, Thomas Hardres, Richard Wilkinson, Thomas Godfrey, Edward Roberts, George Newman, James Newman, Thomas Courtop, Philip Ward, The MAYOR of Rochester".

Thus did the design of this Jewish Lord (who had been disloyal to his King, and treacherous to his Country) vanish into stink, which will remain fresh in the nostrils of fame, and render him odious to his country to latest posterity; which fame was all the reward I ever heard he received from the Committee; and which in my opinion, was no better than that of Erostratus, who wilfully set fire to the temple, that he might be famed when dead.

Now the engagers resolved to regard no obstructions whatever, farther than to kick them out of their way; and accordingly, on Monday morning the horse and foot marched from Canterbury towards Rochester; the foot went to Sittingborne that night, where they quartered; and Colonel Hatton's horse, with the Commissioners, and the rest of the gentlemen, marched in a very orderly and military manner to Rochester.

At Rochester, they met with the gentry of the county from all quarters in as great number, as at a general rendezvous; but the main body of the men they had drawn together, (who came in with a voluntary cheerfulness and great resolution) lay in and about Dartford, as being an advance twenty miles forward of their next day's march to the appointed rendezvous.

That night came several gentlemen out of Essex, to treat with the Commissioners at Rochester, (who were met there from all parts of the county) about the association of both counties in the general engagement, assuring them, that the whole county of Essex, would unanimously rise to join them, and desired a meeting of a party of the Kentish Gentlemen, to join in a parley somewhere over the water, with others that should be selected in Essex for that purpose; but we being then so near the period of that time, wherein by our general engagement we had bound the whole country to meet, and to march towards London, could not engage in any such thing; but took the promise of those gentlemen as an assurance, that the county of Essex, would unanimously concur to rise at the same time, and join with us in the main interest. Others came also from Surrey, to treat on the same terms, promising as great a readiness of that county to join in the association, which was received with great alacrity.

About midnight the same night, (we being to march forwards the next morning) came down a post, with an order from the House of Commons to Rochester, to the Commissioners joined in the engagement, to this purpose.

"That, whereas they did understand, that the people of Kent were coming up to Westminster in a tumultuous and pretended petitionary way, they knew not the intentions of it, and had therefore referred them to treat with their General, the Lord Fairfax, and the Committee of Derby-House."

This rigorous order for preventing their proceeding, being received and read, in the morning the general council being met, the business was debated, when it was found, that the above order had quite turned the balance, and absolutely altered the constitution of the general interest; for they could not but believe, that the army would advance entirely against them, well knowing (considering the posture the country was in) what it would be to treat with a conquering and potent adversary, in the unexperienced condition of a new raised and undisciplined body of raw men.

Upon which, by a general result, orders were immediately dispatched away to Dartford, and the places adjacent, where the main body then quartered, and lay upon guard, to march back to Rochester, having received intelligence, that within a very short time, the Lord Fairfax, with his main body, would advance towards us; however, a guard was left at the place called Stone Bridge, near Gravesend, to secure that passage; the which was defended but a short time, for the enemy (for such we might easily judge them to be by this time, by their seizing all gentlemen and others they met) coming up close, forced their way.

When they came back to Rochester, Mr. Matthew Carter having received commission of a Quarter-Master General of all the forces then raised, or to be raised in that county, for the Commissioners and Gentlemen engaged, received orders from the Council for the quartering them there; whereupon, he first caused them to be drawn up by distinct regiments, in several fields, whereby he was able to take an exact account of the strength of every regiment, so to know how to dispose of them, and inform the Council of their full number, which he mustered in rank and file, completely armed, seven thousand of the infantry, all well accoutered, being most of them very sufficient men of ability, and not wanting of honorable resolutions. The horse being upon parties abroad, and not drawn together, could not be so well taken notice of. At which time, there were also at several places of the county, about three thousand more, which never came up to this party, as at Canterbury, Maidstone, Sittingborne, Sandwich, and Dover. This gallant body, by his care, were equally divided into quarters in Rochester, Strood, and Chatham, and the horse in villages near adjacent; and the engagers now began to join more closely, and taking time by the fore-lock, thought it not good to let slip a minute, lest their hopes and security might be lost with it; and began more seriously to consider, what might probably advance their safety and honor, knowing that what they were now to trust to, was a difficult severity of fortune, the army being likely enough to fall in suddenly upon them.

Amongst many considerations, they at last concluded, that the next business to be undertaken, must be to model that party into a formidable army, and to appoint one particular man to command in chief; for they were now forced to stand upon their guard, to maintain that with their swords, which was intended only in a just and peaceable way, and according to the ancient customs of this kingdom. A sad world, when men shall fall deeper into the pit of destruction, by the endeavours of those they supplicate for aid to bring them out; and who, by natural, as well as legal alliance and interest are bound to assist, and by themselves appointed for it. If this be to reform, heavens preserve all good christians and loyal subjects from reformation.

Sir Thomas Fairfax

Having thus resolved, they appointed a

rendezvous the next day at Barnham Downs, three miles distant from thence, towards Maidstone; where the Lord Norwich was proclaimed General at the head of the army, (for being now drawn together they deserved that title) and the gallant body of infantry received him with the utmost cheerfulness; expressing an unparallel'd willingness to serve their King, and as much joy that they were so engaged to it, knowing that their service was not only for him, but the whole kingdom's peace, the recovery of the liberties of their country, and the tranquillity of the Church of England.

It hath been a general and true observation in all ages and common wealth's, that those who engage in other mens' quarrels, are remiss and inspirited, as knowing that they shall partake in the danger, but not in the victory, since others would receive the greatest and fairest fruit thereof, and likewise arrogate the honor to themselves; whereas they also that take up arms for their country, may conceive better hopes that God will prosper them, because they seek not to take from others, but to keep their own; and they fight not for other men's honor, but their own defence, whereby the whole benefit of the victory will redound to themselves.

This rendezvous being broke up, the army marched again into quarters, though not the same as before, nor by the Quarter-master General's desire, and contrary to the Lord General's sense or intentions, whose advice was, that it would have been most convenient to lodge them close together, or in the field, it being very fair weather.

I have been informed there were some who invented a most detestable aspersion on the Earl of Norwich, by throwing this dirty and odious calumny in the face of his innocent and unspotted fame; "That he was a person who betrayed that service to its succeeding destruction; and that he made it his business to take that command upon him, that he might the more easily effect the design, being himself no soldier."

And so impudently, or ignorantly, they proceeded in this ignoble derogation, as to raise a confirmation of it from this conclusion, that had it not been so, he had certainly lost his life for his loyal service, as well as the Lord Capell, and the Earl of Holland, &c.

First, it was his own inclination which directed him to join with the gentlemen of the engagement, and his coming to Rochester was accidental; as was also his being at Colchester, as I heard him declare; for, being on his journey to Sussex, took that road to avoid the army, who then lay very thick in the other. At the instant he arrived at Rochester, the Commissioners disputing whom to invest with the command, and hearing of his arrival, immediately appointed peculiar gentlemen to make a civil address to him, with the tender of that command, and their serious obedience and service with it, as being a peer of the realm, and a nobleman of so known a worth, and a mind so deep and able, as to capacitate him for any great design. Whereby the strife which threatened destruction, would be ended, being already kindled by sparks of emulation, in the breasts of some gentlemen then interested; having before with much earnestness, solicited the Duke of Richmond to that honorable, though unbeneficial engagement. But his fears turning prophets, dictated to his soul more powerful arguments for a denial.

The answer made by the Earl of Norwich, on the Commissioners begging him to accept the command, follows:

"I am confident the Duke will yet engage with his country, so generally,

Panoramic view of Colchester at the time of the visit of Cosimo, Duke of Tuscany 1669. Note the ruins of St. Mary's Church to the left of the picture.

unanimously, and courageously met; and upon so just, unquestionable, and candid a design; and I believe he will undertake the command."

For the further advancing whereof, he offered himself as a solicitor for them to the Duke; which favour they gratefully accepted, and he as willingly performed: and going to Cobham to him, with his best rhetoric and powerful persuasions, invited and courted him to it, but all to no effect. Whereupon the Commissioners at his return still entreating him, and as it were, pleading the necessity of it to him, he at last accepted of it, to the great content and satisfaction of all the gentry and commonality then met together.

But (as I have heard him declare since) only that the army might be modelled, whereby it might be a greater invitation to the Duke; not that he intended afterwards to desert the service, but continue in it; only with an acknowledgment of superiority in the Duke, for the better encouragement of the army, who must of necessity receive so great and vigorous courage, by being headed and engaged with a generous nobleman.

All persuasions alike in effect, he became totally engaged; which (though he was no soldier) was a prospect as advantageous as could be wished for, had heaven designed it fortunate; for, through the whole course of succeeding service, he most prudently declared himself, and after his own opinion laying it down to a Council of War, for a mature and general result; appearing in his constant actions more of a soldier, than some of considerable figure and undertaking, who have boldly ventured to traduce his loyalty and honor.

This night, the army, by order of some of the Council held in the field, who were more generous spirited gentlemen, than experienced politicians or soldiers, was quartered at large in the country, and the General Commissioners returned back to Rochester, where Sir Anthony Aucher and Mr. Hales left them; not as some falsely furnished and gave out, because they heard of the advance of the enemy, nor through any discontent, as others idly reported; but upon this account; Mr. Hales being of a more noble and virtuous gallantry than his years might speak him to be, living within fifteen miles of Rochester, had upon his first engagement, (as he expressed in my hearing) made a resolution not to see home, till he had seen the army in a formidable posture; according to which resolution he had not, but constantly continued with them till this night; when having seen the army in such a state as that day's rendezvous, and the appointment of a General rendered it, took it for an absolute solution of his engagement; and resolved that night to go home, only to accommodate himself the better with money, and other necessaries for a longer march, and to return the next morning; so taking leave of the General, the Commissioners, and the rest of the gentlemen, rode to his house; and Sir Anthony Aucher, by his earnest entreaty went along with him, but the misfortunes of the succeeding night obstructed their return.

For, in the night, the Lord Fairfax, with his whole body marching down towards Maidstone, and finding the river slightly guarded about Farley Bridge, beyond the town two miles, easily got over; and with a strong party fell upon the town, before those within it were alarmed; in which town were part of Sir John Maynies and Sir William Brockman's regiments, which never came to the rendezvous, consisting of about eight hundred men.

The enemy being possessed of that passage, marched over with their whole body, they in the town not having true intelligence all the day before of them, and fell upon their out-guards so violently, that within a short space, those in the town were forced to fight upon extraordinary disadvantages; the enemy so far exceeding them in number, and the army quartered at such a distance, they could not retreat, nor have relief time enough to assist them. However, their courage was such, as made their enemies know they fought with men, well satisfied in the justice of their cause, not to be daunted or startled at the appearance or apprehension of death, though in never so grim a shape, but rather like true-born heroes, contemning all danger, and death itself, so they might but bury their misfortunes in the wounds of their furious and oppressive enemies; who thinking them no other than a number of men huddled together in a tumultuous manner, because of their being so suddenly gotten together, (the whole body being raised within ten days) fell on them with so much violence, as if they had been lions, and would have devoured them in an instant, or like a boisterous whirlwind scattered them before them like dust; but contrary to their expectations, instead of finding a prey, they met with those that were more likely to make a prey of them, whose bold resolutions soon daunted their fury: and these tumultuous disorderly fellows, (as they termed them) they found orderly enough to oppose them; and although newly raised, yet of courage equal to the oldest soldiers, selling their lives and liberties at as dear a rate as ever men did; few of them falling, without first dispatching twice as many of the others, to receive their reward from their grand Lord and Master, who undoubtedly paid them their arrears in the other world for their faithful and diligent service in this.

This unexpected engagement became very hot, each party contending which should express most valour; the one defending their lives, and disputing their fortifications, which were only bare and thin hedges, with as little thought of danger or security, as if it had been an impregnable fort.

The foes also behaved themselves as gallantly, as if they did not think of a possibility of being beaten. In short, this overpowered party so bravely defended their ground, that they had beaten off their enemy in such a manner, that the Lord Fairfax finding his party in great disorder, even upon a retreat, alighted from his horse and came himself with them, to encourage them on, who were so daunted by the unexpected courage of these defendants, that their disorder had like to have much endangered their whole body.

But at last, a fresh party pouring their shot upon them, they were beaten off from their hedges, and forced to dispute the loss of ground from place to place, against an extraordinary disadvantage; the enemies broke in upon them on all sides, and showed but little remissness in their execution, when they had an opportunity to make home charges upon them; all this while they left not their courage with their ground, but disputed the loss of every foot, with as much resolution as if but beginning to engage, from street to street, porch to porch, often falling upon the enemy's horse with only their swords, in such a gallant manner, as if as prodigal of their bloods as they were of their blows, which they distributed in a plentiful manner on every one who dare stand to receive them; insomuch, that they often put them to retreat by their bold encounters; but being still overpowered by the numerous reserves which continually advanced on them, were forced to continue their retreat, till as last they came to the church-yard, and from thence to the church, quitting not any place dishonorably or unhandsomely: so that they made the engagement so really hot and difficult, that I am confident the victors themselves would have wished to have rather been without that victory, than to have purchased it at so dear a rate. But this party after a long fight, were drawn to so hard a push, as to be forced to capitulate, none coming to their assistance or relief, unless it were a few scattering men, who hearing they were engaged, left their quarters without orders, and huddled into this crowd of confused destruction which they were overwhelmed in.

Some people accuse the General of being treacherous or negligent, for not relieving that party, which they say, might easily have been done; and in all their discourses, endeavour to obscure the face of his honor with black shades of infamy, but all cannot do; his honor was too high, for those short-winged revilers to hurt, having a soul, I am confident, as white with innocent and loyal thoughts as his head with hairs, and a spirit as active as the boldest who dared question it.   And to clear him in this, first, although proclaimed General of that army, yet of so short a date was that title, as that he was not clearly empowered with the charge of them, and the conduct of their interest, as (like a General) to act his own will immediately in it; there being as yet too many Generals, or at least ambitious spirits interested, who having formerly a power in the raising of them, had not yet quite laid down the same, and who supposed nothing must or ought to be done without their opinions; by whose advice and persuasions, the whole body was quartered in the country at large, too wide indeed to be rallied in any considerable time, or drawn to a rendezvous, whatever occasion there might be for them; as was too apparently true here.   It was the advice of the General, to lodge them that night in the field by the river side; and had the gentlemen of the county observed his council, the body had remained entire; waiting for and ready to receive the enemy upon any motion they should make; and the river would have been so guarded, that the enemy could never possibly have forced any place or passage over.   But the men were thought weary, and harassed off their legs, having made very tedious marches; and therefore must have fresh quarters, to revive and refresh their exhausted spirits; by which means the enemy made an easy passage over the river, without any opposition; and the party in the town were quite lost, before the army or a considerable party for their relief could be drawn together to any rendezvous.   And yet not only strangers to the affair, (who certainly ought to be careful how they censure and asperse men of so much honor) but some young soldiers laid the loss of the battle upon the General, who I am assured, all that night while constant alarms were sounded in his ears of their being engaged, did his utmost endeavours to draw parties to a rendezvous from their quarters to their immediate assistance, but none could be forced out; whereupon, early next morning, he caused the army to be got together, and drawn up to a rendezvous at Finsbury Fields, on the other side of the river Medway, by Strood; where a Council was called in the field, and upon a report that it was yet possible to relieve them at Maidstone, it was a general result and desire of the General to march thither.   Upon which, the whole army marched through Rochester, the General being resolved to relieve them if it were possible, or to fight the whole army of the enemy.

But he had not marched two miles, when certain intelligence came, that they were all cut off, and taken prisoners the night before, though many of them came up to the army afterwards, having made their escape.

Upon this intelligence, the army marched back to Rochester, where the General with the Commissioners, called a Council, to consult what measures were best to be taken in their present condition; the Parliament having before-hand refused to receive their Petition, and the enemy already entered the very bowels of their country, and a party roving about, and making a prey of their estates and friends.

Major Osborne, an officer of the Parliament's, with a troop of horse had reached Ashford, and was proceeding towards Sittingborne; upon which, Colonel Hammon was ordered to stay with his regiment at Sittingborne, and Colonel Hatton marched back with his horse, and meeting with this troop of the enemy's, charged them, where Major Summer was killed, and one or two more gentlemen wounded.

Upon this, Sir Richard Hardres was again called back by the Commissioners, into East Kent, to raise the rest of the country, and to take care for the securing of Canterbury and other towns. Sir Michael Lusey, was also raising all the men he could, and Major Osborne with his troop, secured him in it; by which means, the whole country began to show the face of an absolute seat of war. But now the courage of the soldiery at Rochester was such, as would not allow the General time enough to resolve on any thing, being then in consultation what course to steer; for though the weather was such as would have invited them to desire the shelter of the town, rather than expose themselves to such an extremity of rain as then showered down; yet they were so desirous and greedy of action, as almost tended to mutiny; for, drawing out their colours, caused their drums to beat, saying, "If their Officers would not march, they would march and fight without them."

Whereupon, the Earl of Norwich commanded them to be drawn into the field, to rendezvous in the same place as before; not being yet resolved which way to contrive the laying of his design to the best advantage; for he would act nothing without the absolute consent of the Council, in which was now included many able soldiers, who came in from several parts to join and engage with us; more indeed came, than the present condition of the county would permit accommodation for.   This caused an uneasiness in several gentlemen, who coming from London by water, unprovided with horses and accoutrements of war, could not be supplied here, and therefore imagined themselves slighted; which the Commissioners being told of, immediately ordered provision to be made for their maintenance, at the expense of the county, and promised they should be further provided for according to their quality, with all convenient speed; and to encourage them in their loyal designs, Mr. Hales presented them with thirty pounds out of his own pocket, which was distributed amongst them.

It had been the advice of some of the gentlemen concerned, to place the army in this city, and by fortifying the same, defend it as long as they could.   But this scheme was disapproved of by others, who better understood military politics; well knowing that the general engagement was designed for action, and not to lie idle; beside, the river was of itself a fortification for one part of the town.

Wherefore, upon coming into the field, the General summoned a council of the chief officers of the army, and gentlemen; at which it was disputed, whether they should march on towards London, in the prosecution of their intended design, according to the engagement, or march back to fight the enemy, who were wildly roving in the very heart of the country; or by joining with those in East Kent, strengthen their force, and either fight the enemy, or secure that country.   But it was not long, before they concluded to march on; knowing that though their body of infantry was strong enough to face the enemy in the field, if occasion should require it; yet the horse was so weak, as not to enable them to fight at all, having not two hundred horse that they dare put any confidence in; and as for joining with those in East Kent, they were strong enough of themselves; besides, they knew, that if they marched backwards the enemy would certainly come down more powerfully upon them; and by forcing them to retreat into a corner of the country, take off all hopes of assistance from any other county, which they expected, according to the association agreed on betwixt Surrey, Essex and themselves; and if they marched on, they should draw the army after them.   Again, by drawing nearer those two counties, it would be an encouragement and assistance to join them together; who once doing so, would make so great a body, as, in all probability would be formidable to the enemy's; for now they were forced violently into an absolute defensive war.

This being the result of the Council, we immediately marched from the rendezvous towards Dartford; only Colonel D. Wyles, with the chief part of his regiment, marched away towards East Kent, which regiment mustered twelve hundred men.

Colonel Hammon's regiment of foot, lying about Sittingborne and Feversham, were ordered by the General to march back to Canterbury to strengthen that place, and did not come up to the rendezvous.

About midnight we came to Dartford, where the General caused a letter to be drawn up and sent to the Mayor, Aldermen and Common Council of the city of London, to give them notice of our march that way, as also of our intentions, desiring their assistance, which we hoped for, having treated before with them; or at least, that if we might not be assisted, that they would permit us to march through the city to Westminster without interruption or resistance, engaging not to do the least damage.

But they (like a dog to his vomit) were turned to their old course of Parliament service; and no sooner received the letter, but instead of returning a civil answer to the General, dispatched it away to the Speaker of the House of Commons unopened.

However, we knew nothing thereof till the next evening; so we marched on all that night and the next day, without any refreshment or repose. That day about noon, we came to Greenwich, where the General drew the whole army into the park, expecting to receive some satisfaction from the City, as also from Surrey, Southwark and Essex. But we found small encouragement or reason for the continuance of our hopes, receiving no intelligence from Surrey, nor any news of appearance of men for our assistance, either from thence or any other place. London, we heard, had shut up, and guarded her ports against us; only there came a gentleman out of Southwark, who assured the Quarter-master General, that if the General would send any considerable party into the borough of Southwark for their assistance, that they would unanimously rise and join with us; which he acquainted the Lord General with, who returned him this answer.

"That in regard of his being a stranger and not known, he must not expect a party should be sent upon his bare assertion; but if he would return to those gentlemen of the borough, that he said employed him, and if any of the principal men would engage to what he promised, that then they should have what party they desired."

With which answer he returned, but never came back.

There came also a gentleman out of Essex, who assured the General, that the said county was up for to join with us, (which was more than was expected, having heard contrary news at our first coming to the park;) and that about Bow, were two thousand men in arms, and more at Chelmsford. Upon which intelligence, the General (earnestly intending the prosecution of what he had undertaken) crossed the water in the ferry-boat with his horse, and went privately into Essex, not carrying one servant with him, intending to go only to Bow or Stratford, where, his informer assured him, a body was gotten together; and after knowing the truth hereof to return: and that if he found the country in so good a posture as his intelligencer related, upon his return to provide boats, and conduct the army safe over to join with them. He left Sir William Compton, then Major General with the charge of the army, by whose appointment, provision of bread, beer and cheese, was brought into the park, though it proved a great difficulty to obtain it in that town, not being well furnished for its own inhabitants.

Our party was now much weakened from what it was two days before, and no assurance of any friends appearing, we were absolutely frustrated of our design of marching through the city of Westminster. Our condition began to seem somewhat desperate, not knowing what to trust to, beside God's providence; for we were not able to fight with any hopes of victory or success if they had followed us, although so great a resolution was still among us, that had an army of double the enemy's engaged us, it would have proved difficult to have vanquished us.

Night being come, the General did not return according to expectation, nor could he; for, finding no party stirring at Bow or Stratford, he made no stay till he came to Chelmsford, for he would be assured of the condition of that county before he returned, which he intended next morning; and there being no possibility of procuring boats for the transporting such a number of men over in the night, which were the next hopes we had left, some timorous spirits began to steal away, and put such a distraction amongst the whole party, as every man appeared in confusion. To advance which disorder, one riding into the park in the dark of the night, told the soldiers that they were in very great danger; that their Officers wished them to shift for themselves; no man regarding what he was, nor demanded his reason; which so amused the soldiers that heard it, and so encouraged the distraction, (although no enemy was near) that many began to shift for themselves; and procuring a ferry-boat, rowed over the Isle of Dogs to get off; some also endeavouring so to do, were forced back by the soldiers, who exclaimed against them for running away, and threatened to fire at them if they offered to stir off the shore with the boat. Thus did this well-ordered business suddenly suffer, from the unconstant humour of fortune, the greatest change that ever happened. But all men are subject to change, and therefore ought to be the more cautious in prosperity, and resolute in adversity; for too much security in the one, precipitates to the other; and too much dejection and remissness in the other, throws us into despair and destruction.

This unlooked-for distraction, created in some a panic fear, in others a mad fury; so that every man began to shift for himself, and to think of his own security, being doubtful of it in almost every place; but the providential power of All-wise Divinity, who ever prevents our misfortunes, and gives life to future actions, when grounded on religion and honor, did so in this disorderly body, who had thrown themselves into the very mouth of destruction, and who otherwise might have been secure enough, and remained where they were till the General's return.

The greatest part of the foot, and a few of the horse transported themselves from several places, over the River Thames, no man knowing what would be the event of their rashness; nor were they able to give a reason for what they did. However, it proved lucky enough in the end, for had we remained there till the General's return, (according to the condition we found the Essex people in) he would scarce have laid the scene of his designs that way; by which means we had lost the service which afterwards accrued, and should have fallen instantly into dishonor.

But this rashness had been ill enough too, had not the great All-seeing Soul of nature, enlivened our then almost dead fortunes, by a miraculous guide through the gulph of misery we were plunged into: for having thus confusedly thrown ourselves over to the opposite side of the Thames for our further safety, fearing danger without cause, we had no sooner landed there, but supposing ourselves to have been in Essex (where then our only hopes were anchored) we were unexpectedly deceived, by finding ourselves in Middlesex, under the hamlets of the tower, and, were hurrying ourselves to absolute ruin; and, like the unfortunate vessel, seeking to avoid the fatal rock of Scilly, plunged herself into the more desperate gulph of Charibas.

Here (by the appointment of the House) lay a regiment of hambleteers of the tower, drawn up to their arms in several guards, ready to receive and cut us off at our landing, which was easy enough to perform, considering the disorder we were then in; every man marching according to his own humour, and came up from the river's side, at several places, and divers ways.

But Sir William Compton (a man truly noble, and more complete in gallantry, virtue and honor than years) having first discovered this plotted mischief, and perceiving the ruin we were running blindfold into, treated with them for the whole party, before he would permit any man to march in amongst them; which he imagined, would be the only way to proceed, our present condition duly considered. By which means, articles were drawn up and signed by him and the Officers in chief of the regiment; which were,

"That all our foot should lay down their arms, and depart to their own homes, or where they pleased quietly, without having any violence or molestation offered to them; and all gentlemen and officers, with their horses and arms, to march where they pleased without any disturbance."

But those conditions were almost as soon broken as made; for, before the foot came up, some gentlemen marching through the guards, had their horses and arms both taken from them by the Major of the regiment, by whom the articles on their part were signed.

Then the foot, and a great number of gentlemen, by their easy march coming up together, and understanding what had been done, and how unlikely those were to keep articles, when they should lie unarmed at their mercy, who had so unworthily begun, and so soon broke them, marching through two or three guards, no man being permitted to pass any by-way, by reason of the easy march the gentlemen made; the foot came closer up, so that they hoped to avoid the abuses of those who began to scoff and jest at them.

And considering what a state an inauspicious fate had reduced us to, and these gallants having broke their conditions, we then began to think of some other way than to disband, and submit ourselves to such worthless wretches, who were void of honor; and enquiring into the dispositions of the private soldiers, found them resolute enough to express themselves rather desirous of dying there, in the bed of honor, than to survive such an infamous misfortune, and become slaves all the remainder of their days. This bold resolution proved the happy guide to a better fate; and all concluded to make a second dispute for conditions and to charge through them: and being now in the midst of them, every man provided himself accordingly; the foot all lighting their matches, and the gentlemen drawing their pistols, began to alter the constitution of our jeering hambleteers, who left their boasting; and we marched on from guard to guard through the midst of them, as if moving to the place of disbanding, where we expected an opposition, and were fully resolved to force through it; but the last and most distant guard was placed just at Bow town; who beholding us marching and getting ourselves into better order, were absolutely discountenanced from a thought of opposition; so we marched on without the least affront, till we came to Bow-Bridge, where we supposed was the place for our disbanding; at the further end of which bridge was a turnpike, strongly guarded with musqueteers, and having entered upon the bridge, we made a stand to parly with them; but after a short discourse, and asking whether they were friends or foes? we were answered from them, friends: whereupon we replied, If you are friends, let your turnpike be opened; so they opened their turnpike, and with a very great shout let us in. Now being in Essex, we marched clear through these hambleteers, and carried away the Major prisoner, and another officer; but afterwards, upon their paroles, they were suffered to go to London, but never returned again according to their engagements, by which you may guess how little honor they had in them: thus we marched on till we came to Stratford, where we met with the General again, returning back to us, in expectations of finding us in the same posture he left us in, in the park at Greenwich: and on being acquainted with what had been done, seemed much troubled, and knowing the long and tedious marches we had made, that the preceding night's action could not permit any repose, and that we had received no refreshment for two nights, immediately gave command for the drawing us up into order on the green, and for such refreshment to be procured as the place would afford for the present, before we marched any further.

This must be agreeable to the will of Providence, for had we received the least affront or opposition from the hambleteers, or by any other obstruction, hindered ever so little time, we had been absolutely cut off; or had we disbanded, we had been as suddenly ruined; for, we had no sooner marched over the bridge, and scarce drawn up, but we received a very strong alarm from a party of Colonel Whaley's horse; who, it was conceived, came thither purposely on the intelligence that we were to disband, to make a prey of us when naked, and by surprising us, make what spoil they pleased with the private soldiers, and to take all the gentlemen prisoners; but, by God's assisting providence that was prevented; and now they thought to have beat us off from our guards by their appearance only; for they marched on in full career, (having laid an ambuscade of dragoons to secure their retreat) as if they would have destroyed us in a minute; which indeed had been accomplished, if we had been as tame as they supposed us to be: but being aware of their design, we roused our men from the drowsy spirit which possessed them; and a party of foot being drawn out to strengthen the guard, and a party of horse to the number of thirty, marching from the turnpike, gave them a home charge, which startled them, and put them to a complete rout in an instant, and killed and wounded many of them; which successful action gave life to our fatigued spirits, and encouraged one party so much that they followed the pursuit as far as Mile-End Green, where they fell into the ambuscade, who fired upon them from the hedges, so they were forced to make great speed in retreating; though none pursued. In which service, only one gentleman, a Grecian, being shot by the dragooners was left behind upon the green; and in the charge, Captain John Lynn was cut across the chin and over the breast, which was all the hurt we sustained in it: but although our pursuit continued no farther, yet the enemy kept on their flight in great disorder, which, as I was informed, gave an alarm to the whole city, as far as Temple-Bar.

After this, the hambleteers began to oppose us, but were soon forced to take sanctuary in Bow Church, where we surrounded them by a party of horse and foot, and obliged them to treat with us for a quiet returning home to their own houses, engaging themselves never to oppose us again. This was a very surprising change of fortune in two opposite parties in less than two hours time!

Then our party again retired within the turnpike, and strong guards commanded on all passes and fords about the river, and on all highways and avenues for hindering the enemy from making any incursions upon us, who were again summoning and drawing up a strong guard at Mile-End Green, both of horse and dragoons.

Our party now thought of resting a little, and then begin again; as thinking themselves secure from any opposition or inconveniency, being among our professed friends; when our condition met with another reverse, and was more likely to change for the worse than before. For after we had run through so many difficulties, and were wearied out with tedious marches, our soldiers seemed almost ready to fall down in the street for want of food to sustain them; we were like to fall into another encounter with adverse fortune. The General, notwithstanding his great age, which might easily have disenabled him from such toil, yet as if he had been absolutely indefatigable, or else miraculously nourished, (not having received any rest or sleep for the space of four days and three nights, and yet not seemed to want any) posted immediately to Chelmsford, where the gentry of the country were met; giving orders for quartering our shattered army in Stratford till other orders from him; and our Quarter-master General Carter sent for the Constable and gave orders accordingly; the Constable went in obedience to his warrant, but soon returned again, accompanied with three or four Justices of the Peace for that part of the county, who began to question the authority of the Quarter-master General in quartering an army in that country, intimating that they were all very quiet before, and in friendship with the Parliament; adding, that the Parliament had granted them what they desired, and had sent them an Act of Indemnity, but that our bringing an army into their county, would draw down the Parliament's upon them and make it a seat of war; and therefore they could not any way condescend that we should fix our quarters there; it not being for their safety, but on the contrary, the readiest way to destruction.

These were not cheerful expressions to men who had run through so many hazards and difficulties. Having left our own country to the cruelty of a most barbarous enemy, to come agreeable to an associated engagement to their assistance, and by which we hoped to be strong enough to break the bonds and tear off the shackles from our most inhumanly imprisoned sovereign, and enslaved countrymen; and were no sooner entered the confines of their county, (from whence so many public declarations of their loyal and sincere intentions had flown abroad through the whole kingdom, and who had so lately checked the insolence of their proud enemy, and prevented their forcing a violent incursion upon it) but to have such an unexpected welcome, was too harsh and severe, and might have proved of mischievous consequence, if resented by the inferior sort of the army, whose fury is not easily pacified, when inflamed with so just a discontent.

Upon which, the Quarter-master General returned the following answer:

"That as to the power by which he quartered that army, it was by commission of the General, and that he quartered them in that place by immediate command also from him; and, that as to our coming into that country, it concerned him not to dispute it; neither could he give any other account than the engagement between those counties, and their General, the Earl of Norwich. And if they wanted any further satisfaction in their desires, they must receive it from the Lord General himself."

The General being gone to Chelmsford, Sir William Compton, Major General, hearing of the dispute, came also to them, and gave the like satisfaction, but would not stay long with them, not knowing them, nor by what authority they were empowered to make these interrogatories.

Our bloods yet hardly cool since the last affront, were heated again by this new one, and the consideration of the sad success of our just and honorable designs, were resolved to quarter here till receiving further orders from the General; and if the disposition of the country should prove contrary to our hopes, and the expectations of the whole kingdom (agreeable to the expressions of those men of Belial) to march on, forcing our way through all obstructions till we found a party to join with us, or to be destroyed in the field, thereby winning an honorable liberty, or a tomb.

Here we quartered till Wednesday afternoon, it being Sunday morning when we came thither, still keeping the enemy in play, who lay with his guards within half a mile of us, and their scouts incommoding us at the end of Bow. All which time the Earl of Norwich continued at Chelmsford, forwarding the business with the gentlemen of the county, who had not long before published their declaration, as follows:

THE ENGAGEMENT, OR DECLARATION OF THE GRAND JURY, FREEHOLDERS AND OTHER INHABITANTS OF THE COUNTY OF ESSEX, IN PROSECUTION OF THEIR LATE PETITION, PRESENTED TO BOTH HOUSES OF PARLIAMENT.

"We the Grand Jury, Freeholders and other Inhabitants of the said county in the prosecution of the said Petition, do engage ourselves one to another, and declare,

I. That we will not pay any Excise or other Taxes, till all the desires in our said Petition be obtained by us.

II. That we admit of no soldiers to come into our county, but such as agree with us in our said Petition, and in this engagement.

III. That we will employ our utmost endeavours to preserve and defend our Royal King CHARLES, his kingly Government; and the Subjects' Liberty; That is to say, the Common and Statute-Laws, and will never submit ourselves to any other kind of laws, much less to any arbitrary power whatsoever.

IV. That we will protect and defend one another, and all that shall adhere to us in the pursuance, performance, and keeping of this engagement: and if any inhabitant of our county shall refuse to join with us herein, we shall esteem him a person disaffected to the peace and welfare of the same.

Notwithstanding this engagement, they were backward enough in prosecuting any thing serviceable, agreeable to their Petition. When his Excellency came, he found the greatest part of the gentry of the county met; but affairs were so disordered and confused, that there seemed almost an impossibility of any good to proceed from that mountainous conception and promises: and our party threatened to cut in pieces by a cruel enemy who were already possessed of our whole county, had ruined our friends, made lavish havoc of our estates, and ourselves were proclaimed traitors, for coming hither to their assistance.

The disorder was so great, that the Gentlemen and Commoners, who came there with intent to prosecute their Petition and Engagement, were likely to have dispersed forthwith; Captain Lynn, of that country, had once before raised a thousand men, who were immediately dispersed. An order of indemnity being read at the head of them by Colonel Farre, the Committee of the county so pressed it to them that they went all quietly home. And now were active in their endeavours for the ruin of the main intent of the design; as indeed it concerned them enough, well knowing, that the prosperity of loyalty is destruction to rebellion.

They were active in their machivilian stratagems for countermining all policy against them, but Sir Charles Lucas, was there earnestly tending upon the design, with many other gentlemen for the good of the King, and advancement of the liberty of their country, which was their sole end, and consequently ought to be prosecuted with vigour, thinking by the hazard of a war, we might attain the happy blessing of an honorable and lasting peace. Some thought it best to depart privately from the town, lest an unexpected incon-veniency should arise, and occasion their persons to be seized whereby the general interest would be overwhelmed, the which they began to fear.

But some of the country gentlemen then met together in the said town, desired Sir Charles Lucas, not to go away in that manner, for let the Committee do what they would, they were sensible enough they had ruined and undone them, and that they should no longer abuse them; and that if he would be pleased to draw them out into the field, and stay with them, they would one and all engage with him, and live and die in that engagement, according to the intention of their meeting together; hav-ing resolved not to return till they had performed some loyal act.

Sir Charles Lucas

This sudden change, in a little time, proved very violent, for they im-mediately drew into the field, seized on the Committee, and were so furiously incensed against them, that some of them would immediately have killed them, had not other gentlemen &c. rescued them, pacified the heat of others, and afterwards placed a guard over them; being now resolved, that since they had actually engaged themselves, they would not be obstructed in their prosecution by those grand opposers; who they well knew would be active enough in their endeavours to destroy the design, the actors against them, being complete Committee-men, and of the Parliament's own bringing up, as appeared afterwards by Sir Thomas Honywood, always an enemy to the King and kingdom, who being at liberty, and at his house at Coggeshall, made himself really appear so now, by raising as many horse and foot, as by his power and interest he could draw together, either for love or fear, and made his house a garrison to oppose the country, as much as in him lay, in their proceedings in that loyal design; but this party proved so inconsiderable that it could do but little injury.

The business coming to this height, his Excellency the Lord Norwich, sent his orders to Sir William Compton, to march away for Chelmsford; accordingly we marched away from Stratford with our whole party, which by this time were well recruited, with many men who came up, and divers youths from London, who daily enlisted themselves.

On Wednesday night, we met the General at Rumford, but the enemy coming after us, so obstructed our march, by alarming us in the rear, that the next morning, though the enemy dare not venture to fall upon our rear guard.

The next day, being the 8th of June, we marched on towards Brentwood, whither Sir Charles Lucas was advanced with parties of horse and foot, to join with us: and having intelligence how the enemy followed us with alarms in our rear, commanded all the horse that were then in the town to assist us; so we marched up, and quartered that night at Brentwood, and the next day we marched to Chelmsford, where the Lord Capell, the Lord Loughborow and divers gentlemen of quality from Hertfordshire, and other counties, joined also with us; which gave great encouragement to our army. There also came in a party of about fifty gentlemen, who signing their combination in London, made their rendezvous at Hyde-Park Corner, and marching all the night before, intended to beat up a quarter of the enemies at Epping in their way, but the party was drawn out near the town upon some other design, which disappointed them of their stratagem; so they marched on, and being well mounted, charged through the enemy, and the next day joined us, having lost only one man and one horse; which horse being taken by a countryman was recovered again, as was afterwards the rider.

That afternoon both parties of Kentish and Essex were drawn out to a rendezvous in New-Hall Park, near Chelmsford, then belonging to the Duke of Buckingham. This general meeting gave much encouragement to both parties; and the General and Sir Charles Lucas joined in consultation with the gentlemen of both counties, whereby there was a unity in the engagement, as well as the interest, and the greater hopes of success.

At which council it was once resolved to have marched away immediately, and fallen upon the party of Sir Thomas Honywood's at Coggeshall; but upon a more serious deliberation it was otherwise agreed, and orders given out for quartering in the town that night; but this party of Coggeshall so much discouraged the country, that they began to be very slack in their appearance to join us, and the reverse of what they were at our first arrival; not only by reason of Sir Thomas Honywood's activeness, but because the enemy had entered into the country with their whole body.

On Saturday, the 10th we marched on towards Braintree, taking Leeds-House in our way, which belonged to the Earl of Warwick; where we were opposed by some people who were placed there; and upon the Quarter-master General's coming up to secure it from the violence of the soldiers, they refused to open their gates, being about twelve or fourteen men with fire-arms, &c. who said, that they were placed there for the security of that house, and they would rather die than deliver it up to be plundered. But on being informed that the General himself was coming, and that the Quarter-master General was commanded before to secure them from injury, they gave him entrance with some other gentlemen, imagining it would be of small benefit to dispute with an army.

About noon, the General and Sir Charles Lucas arrived, and after dinner seized on the armory, where they found a good magazine, both of arms and ammunition of all sorts; we carried from thence two brass field pieces, and about two or three hundred muskets and as many pikes, with about sixty great saddles and body arms proportionable to them, and some pistols and carbines, and a good proportion of match and ball, with divers other instruments and furniture of war; also left many of the saddles behind for want of carriages for them. Here we rendezvoused all the afternoon till towards night, in the park beyond the house; the enemy rendezvousing also with a party of theirs very near the other side, and at night in the park; but ventured not to appear all the day in sight of our army.

There was a party of horse also came in to us upon the march, which we supposed at first an enemy, from Hertfordshire and Bedfordshire, consisting of about an hundred and twenty.

From thence we marched forwards, and quartered that night at Braintree; where the next day, being Sunday, both parties were drawn into the field in the forenoon to rendezvous; and after prayers, all the gentlemen that were in the army, were drawn into troops, under the command of the Lord Norwich, Lord Capell, the Lord Loughborow, and Sir Charles Lucas; that they might know how to dispose of themselves upon any occasion of alarm; for being in order, it would be very convenient for quartering them upon every remove.

Here follows an exact Relation of the Expedition of the TOWN of COLCHESTER.

On Sunday, **June the 11th, 1648,** about nine o'clock at night, our party marched from Braintree, and came within six miles of Colchester, on Monday about four in the afternoon, where we halted; Sir Charles Lucas, having received intelligence that they would not receive him in arms; upon which, himself with some other gentlemen, marched at the head of the army, after a party was dispatched away; but before the Quarter-master General left them, to go to the town, intelligence came from the party, that the town stood upon their guard, and were so far from giving entrance to our party, that they opposed them, and were too strong for them: on receipt of which news, Sir Charles, and the gentlemen with him, set spurs to their horses and galloped full speed till they came to the town, when they found the gates shut, and about sixty horse were drawn out in a very formal troop, well armed and accoutered, and some of their scouts were without the turnpike by the Alms-Houses. Sir Charles made a stop here, and sent back a messenger to the army, to hasten their march; but four or five gentlemen keeping on their speed, drew their swords, and charged up to the party, and forced them within the turnpike, so they retreated to Head-Gate, where the whole troop was drawn up in order; and the gentlemen retreated again towards the turnpike; in which fray, one person on horseback, was shot by one of the gentlemen, and fell down dead.   Now the town's-people perceiving the body of the army coming, and that Sir Charles Lucas had drawn up two or three troops of horse very near them, they sent out to treat with him; and upon his engagement that the town should not be plundered, nor any injury offered to the inhabitants for what they had done, they submitted themselves, and engaged to deliver up their horse and arms, with the town; so the gates were opened, and the army quartered that night in the town.

The next day, being Tuesday, June the 13th, about noon, we received a strong alarm, that the enemy were advanced within a mile of the town; and indeed by that time we could find parties, and sent them forth, their forlorns were engaged with our out-guards in the suburbs; which guards were immediately doubled, and it was not long before we were as ready to receive them, as they to assault us: our men being drawn up to their colours, fresh parties were sent out to assist the guards, both of horse and foot; and the enemy came on strongly on all parts of that side of the town next Lexden, and fired up to the very hedges and guards of our foot, but were as furiously opposed, till at last, some of the guards wanting ammunition to maintain the heat of the service, about the Alms-Houses, and the house, called Grimstone's House, were over-powered with the number of men, who threw in their shot like hail upon them, and were forced to retreat, and give the enemy the

Sir Harbottle Grimston

liberty of possessing themselves of all that ground: in which retreat, they upon our guards near Sheer-Gate; where-upon the out-guards were ordered to retire within the town, it being the best policy to take the greatest advantage in opposing an enemy, were the army double the strength of the enemy's; but before this retreat could be made, and the guards drawn within the gates, the dispute grew close and very hot; the enemy coming on so violently, that it was much difficulty to maintain any ground against them, yet were they still resolutely opposed, and it was a hard matter to judge, which showed most courage, the enemy in assaulting, or our party in defending.

Now, we being forced to retreat, although as much out of policy, as danger, gave an encouragement to the enemy to prosecute their charge upon us, thinking themselves more than half victors, already, and that they should in a short time make themselves masters both of the town and us.

But this new army of countrymen, added fire to the heat of the service to such a degree, and with so undaunted a resolution, (far contrary to the enemy's expectation though they had received an experimental knowledge of them at Maidstone) that numbers, not digesting it, left their bodies in the streets and hedges, as infallible witnesses of what had been done: yawning out their souls to receive their arrears in another world, for their religious rebellion in this.

Colonel William Maxey and son.

Many of their dead bodies were thrown into wells, some buried in ditches, others were carried off, and considerable numbers were left behind; their whole loss amounted to upwards of seven hundred men; among whom were Colonel Needham, and divers other prime officers, besides many were wounded, and above one hundred and thirty were taken prisoners, and brought into the town; for having retired within the walls, our shot fell in so thick amongst them, that they could not hold out long; and after seven or eight hour's fighting, they were so disabled, that they were forced to a dishonorable retreat, leaving behind them one brass piece of ordnance, (which they brought to force open the gate) twelve of their train horses, who were shot within twenty yards space of ground, and above five hundred arms, which the next morning were brought into the town.

Their retreat was in such disorder, that had we sallied out with a fresh party upon them, as was once intended, we had cut their whole army off, or at least, the greatest part, as many of them owned.

I must confess, I never saw any men fight with more gallant resolution and courage, than those men did, although raw country fellows; but then how could they do otherwise, having such rare precedents, as those honorable lords and gentlemen, under whose conduct they were brought thither, and whose command they then fought, who ceased not themselves to act the duty of the meanest and inferior officers, and ran the hazard of the most private soldier; they took their pikes in their hands, when their horses were not of immediate service, to give encouragement to the most inferior sort, left by the heat of service, they might grow slow and dull in the performance of their utmost duty.

The Lord Capell charged at Head-Gate, where the enemy were most pressing with a pike, till the gate could be shut, which at last was fastened with his cane only: the enemy were gallant enough too, endeavouring to force their entrance in upon us, and entered so far as to fire under the gate, and several times threw stones over it.

In this engagement we lost Sir William Campion and Colonel Cooke, men of incomparable and unblemished honor, both receiving mortal wounds with shot, upon the first charge in the suburbs, also one Lieutenant, and about thirty or forty private soldiers, and many more wounded.

Sir William Layton, though not interested in any immediate command in the army, yet was of so high and noble a soul, as could not admit of a private engagement in so general a design without assisting, took the charge of an out-guard, and endeavouring to retreat, when he perceived the enemy had surrounded him, was unfortunately shot in the foot; so that before he could recover the gate, it was shut, and the enemy intermixed with his party; insomuch, that he could by no means escape being taken; when a soldier, who had formerly served four years under him, in the King's service, and in his own company, came to him, and would have carried him off, but was forced by reason of the shot that came thick upon them from the town, to run away and leave him; and Sir William was grown so stiff with loss of blood, that he could not shift for himself. After a while, the soldier coming again, carried him off, and secured him from the most inhuman usage of other soldiers; which soldier afterwards proved very serviceable to him, and got him conducted home.

Lieutenant Colonel George Rawlins commanded another out-guard on that part of the town, and was also surprised before he could make his retreat, with about forty foot soldiers; so that in all about eighty prisoners were taken of ours; but many of them who were taken upon this confused retreat, got from them again, and came safe into the town.

Night coming on, and it proving darkish, they made use of the opportunity for re-treating, but before they drew off, set fire on some houses near Head-Gate,

Sir William Campion

hoping thereby that the wind would so force the fire inwards, that it might burn the whole town; but the diligence of the soldiers proved as great in defending it from fire, as before from plunder and the sword, guarding it from an enemy merciless in the one, and insatiable in the other, as the suburbs of the town witnessed; the people whereof, chiefly poor weavers, rather seemed to oppose us, than to assist or help us in all we did; yet the next morning, we found scarce a house unplundered, from the one end to the other, and many poor men dead in their houses, and the women and children fled.

Amongst the rest, myself received this account the next morning by break of day. Just over against the Alms-Houses lived a poor weaver, whose dwelling I happened to ride by, and seeing a woman heavily bemoaning herself, demanded the cause of so much grief; whereupon she answered me, that the last night some of the soldiers who fought against the town, came violently into her house and took what they pleased; and that they were no sooner gone, but others came in, and not finding anything left in the house that pleased them, came to her husband at work in the loom, and demanded money of him, who told them, that he had been worth but little, and that what he had, the soldiers that came before them had taken from him, excepting only a small sum in his purse, which he would willingly give them if they would be satisfied with it; but that not answering their expectations, they told him he was a cavalier rogue, and had more money, which they would have, or kill him; both which he denying, one of them shot him through the body, so that he died immediately: at which noise his son coming in, they fell to cutting of him, and had so cruelly wounded him, that he lay more likely to die than live many days.

But to return; having made their retreat in the night, the next morning they drew back to Lexden, a village about a mile from the town, and cast up a fort just upon the highway to secure the head-quarters, and barricadoes cross all the highways; here they lay about two days quiet, then approaching nearer in the night, cast up another fort in that road towards the town, where they placed a guard; and the next night they entered ground upon a hill called the Warren, and placed a strong guard there the night following, and so every night broke up fresh ground in several places, which they thought most advantageous, running their line by degrees from one redoubt and fort to another.

This gave us just occasion to believe that they intended to plant themselves before us for a longer continuance than before we had imagined, and to block

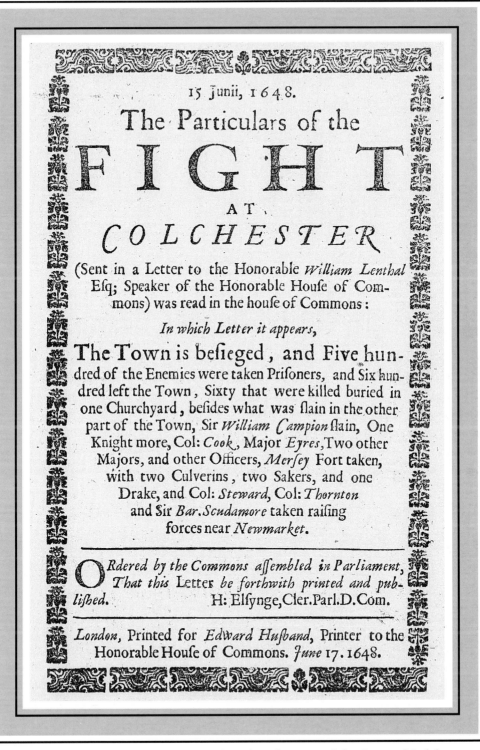

15 Junii, 1648.

The Particulars of the

FIGHT

AT

COLCHESTER

(Sent in a Letter to the Honorable *William Lenthal* Esq; Speaker of the Honorable House of Commons) was read in the house of Commons:

In which Letter it appears,

The Town is besieged, and Five hundred of the Enemies were taken Prisoners, and Six hundred left the Town, Sixty that were killed buried in one Churchyard, besides what was slain in the other part of the Town, Sir *William Campion* slain, One Knight more, Col: *Cook*, Major *Eyres*, Two other Majors, and other Officers, *Mersey* Fort taken, with two Culverins, two Sakers, and one Drake, and Col: *Steward*, Col: *Thornton* and Sir *Bar. Scudamore* taken raising forces near *Newmarket.*

ORdered by the Commons *assembled in Parliament*, *That this* Letter *be forthwith printed and published.* H: Elsynge, Cler.Parl.D.Com.

London, Printed for *Edward Husband*, Printer to the Honorable House of Commons. *June* 17. 1648.

One of the many tracts or letters produced at the time of the Siege of Colchester us up; by which we were invited to consider for our own future security, which then consisted in the greatest care for victualling and fortifying; the only two things to be first thought on in such a cause; especially in a town then defective in both. A place, I suppose, never intended for what it was afterwards ordered to; no man, I think, who had surveyed it with the judicious eye of an experienced soldier, could be so weak as to suppose it a place fitting to be mantled, or maintained as a garrison; for it was our first intentions, only to quarter at Colchester for a night or two, agreeable to the resolution of a council held at Braintree, and conformable to the desire of Sir Charles Lucas, who imagined we might there raise many recruits.

But this engagement having forced us to it, every man enlivened with an active and cheerful behaviour, to forward and advance all things requisite for the business, for march away now we could not, having no way to proceed, without falling into a champion country, where the enemy being very strong, and we unavoidably weak in horse, would have cut us off in an instant; our foot being no such experienced soldiers as to maintain a charge of themselves, against both horse and foot, without hedges to guard and shelter them from the horse.

By the incomparable diligence of all parties, (no man at the first knowing where to find provision of any sort, more than belonged to every private family for their ordinary sustenance) we found in a short time in several places of the town, and particular a place called the Hythe, many private stores of corn and wine of all sorts, with much salt, some fish and a good quantity of powder, the want whereof would suddenly have thrown us into absolute ruin, having very much exhausted our magazine by the last day's business.

It is said, "He who would picture war must first begin with the belly." Accordingly we having many bellies to feed, and not knowing how long it should please God to continue us here, were the most inquisitive after provision; by which means, at the Hythe, we found greater assistance than indeed we could have hoped for, which was conveyed into the town with expedition and secrecy, the enemy being so favourable as not to endeavour to cut us off from that place, till we had almost drained the honey from the comb; which they might easily have done, had they knew what we were doing.

A providence almost as great as that of the Israelites in the Wilderness: and in the memory of man, there never was known such plenty of all things at the Hythe as there was at that time.

Whilst we were thus active for the preventing dangers which might happen, by strengthening the walls of the town, and fortifying those places where no wall was, by casting up ramparts and counterscarps, as a great part of the town required; the enemy was as busy without in running their trenches, making their approaches, and casting up forts and batteries against us; and we as diligent and laborious within, as in truth, not without necessity on our part, the town being in all places very weak, neither had it any more than one flanker about it, and that very bad too, which was called the Old Fort.

Now if it should be objected, why all this time, not being certain of relief, we did not draw out and fight with them, as hath been often urged: they who will judge discreetly of our condition, may be well satisfied of it; we had hopes of speedy relief, both from the Scots and divers other places, who were at the same time in action: besides, it was judged the greatest piece of policy, to keep the enemy in a lingering action, to give a remora to their designs, and ruin them by long delays; by which means, we should gain liberty, and an opportunity to others who were then in action, to work their designs without interruption, and not to run the hazard of an immediate ruin by giving them battle; for, had we fought with them, it must have been upon infinite disadvantages, as I said before First, in the inequality of the number of infantry. Secondly, because we had no

St. Leonard's Church at the Hythe, Colchester

considerable party of cavalry in respect of theirs, whose greatest strength consisted in horse: and it was no rash or fond supposition to think, that could we hold what we had till the rest of the kingdom should rise, we should then do as good service as the immediate victory; we supposed we might possibly hold out a month, and were resolved on it, though it concluded in our own ruin; by which time, if not sooner, we could not but expect to be relieved.

By this design, we were also certain to give liberty to the Scots to march quietly into the kingdom, being then most assuredly upon their march, and near the borders.

Neither was this all the hopes we cherished by this resolution, for there remained a possibility of a victory over that army, by delaying to fight with them, till some more fit opportunity should offer itself; or the tediousness of the service weaken them by hard duty, constant action, and unseasonable lying in the field, in respect of the weather, of which we had many gallant examples. Pompey was well advised for a while, when he refused to fight, and gave Caesar ground; but, when by the importunity of his captains, he ventured upon the battle at Pharsalia, he lost the fame, the freedom of Rome, and thereby his own life.

The Constable of France frustrated the mighty preparation of Charles the Vth. when he invaded Provence, by wasting the country, in forbearing to fight the Duke of Alvaria; by the same policy wearied out the French King in Naples, and dissolved the mighty army of the Prince of Orange in the Low Countries.

One more example I shall insert, touching those hot-spur politicians, who have violently criticised upon that point, and refer the application, by looking into the battle of Pavy, both tragical and fatal to France; where the French King was taken prisoner, and the French frustrated of their main hopes in Italy.

The day before this overthrow, the King summoned a great Council of War, and desired the opinion of his officer, whether he should give a field to the enemy or not: at which an old Captain began to persuade the King to stay, and delay engaging, till supplies, which were already levied, should come and strengthen his army, desiring him not to run hazards, when the welfare of France was at stake; urging, his advice was not only for the King's honor, but for his safety; there was also at the council a young hot-spur Officer, fitter to begin than continue a charge, who alleged, that nothing was more honorable, than gaining a victory by fighting, &c. At the same time, jeering the old Captain; by saying, it was no wonder that an old man should be fearful, and seek delays, whose mind being disturbed with it's usual fears, was endeavouring to find a passage through his guts: the old man could not bear his scurrility; but replied, seeing the King will have us fight, I will die to-morrow an honorable death before his face: when thou, forgetful of thy brags and rashness, shall forsake the field: which prophecy, in all respects, was fulfilled, the field desperately lost, and the King taken prisoner, many more examples of the same nature, I could insert, but think it as unnecessary, as tedious.

And here, though we gave them no field-battle, yet we suffered them not to lie idle from constantly fighting in one place or other, both night and day: neither were they so weak, as some suppose, after our shattering them; for they were in foot, still about or equal our number, before the Suffolk people joined them, who lay upon the bridges of the river so strong before the enemy drew them over, that we could not have forced our passage, in case we had attempted it, without being attacked by the enemy in the rear, and forced to engage both ways, to the hazard of immediate destruction or our whole army.

About the 20th day of June, divers gentlemen were dispatched privately, with Commissions to raise men in Norfolk, Suffolk, and Cambridgeshire; but the country forces having broke up the bridges, and guarded the passes, and the enemy taken the fort, called Mersea Fort, which commanded the passage into that island, there was no passage left open for them, so they were forced to return back, which they did securely, although through the enemy's quarters, not a man being taken.

The next night, parties of horse and foot were commanded to go into the hundred of Tendring, for the bringing in of provisions, which returned the day following, with about an hundred sheep, and sixty oxen; which were all delivered to the Commissary for the general store, and so in like manner, provisions were brought to the public store-houses every night.

Two or three days after this, part of the country rose to join with us; but the Captain, who by commission from Sir Charles Lucas, was to levy and command them, would have betrayed them to their enemy in their rising; in order to ingratiate himself with the prevailing power, (an epidemical disease in this kingdom) but his design, having not so much policy as villainy, was discovered, and himself seized on by the countrymen, till Sir Charles Lucas's pleasure should be further known concerning him, and them; to whom they sent two sufficient men of their party, to give him an account of the affair, making it their earnest request, that he would send a party of horse and foot to assist them in their rising, and to conduct them safe into the town, and accordingly, a party was drawn out, and marched away in the night, who stayed there about a week, and then returned safe with what men they had raised, through the quarters of the Suffolk foot, who were drawn over the river, and encamped betwixt them and the town.

Another party was commanded out in the night, which marched out at the North-Gate, forced through their quarters, and in the morning returned safe, losing not above two men, for which loss they gained livelihood for many more, by bringing in with them above fifty oxen and cows, besides sheep, some corn, and other provisions, and might have brought more; but Sir Charles Lucas being tender of injuring his countrymen, would not permit them to drive from any, but those he knew to be actual enemies; though his tenderness proved a very great inconveniency and prejudice to us in the town; for after that time, we never obtained the like opportunity, the enemy drawing immediately nearer upon us, confined us within narrow bounds, being much incensed with anger in themselves, that they should suffer us to march through their quarters upon a sally, and return again safe. We yet secured the Hythe, as a final refuge for provision, from whence we conveyed daily such necessaries as it would afford, by keeping a constant guard there; which the enemy did not endeavour to hinder us of, till we had left remaining there but little for use.

On the 5th of July, the Council published a proclamation, for calling all such townsmen, as would serve upon the line for the security of the town, to enlist themselves for the service under the several captains and officers, who should be deputed by Sir Charles Lucas to command them, and all others, to bring in their arms to be delivered into the magazine; and that those who refused to enlist themselves should not keep any arms in their houses, on pain of death, and forfeiture of their goods to the benefit and use of the town.

About this time, the enemy encroached so near upon us by their approaches, notwithstanding our daily sallies and skirmishes with them in all parts, that they fell into East-Street, and seized the mill on the river, and placed a strong guard there, which guard (in hopes of firing all that part of the street betwixt them and the town, because many of our men both quartered and guarded there also) set fire to a Tanner's house and barn, and consumed all the goods, leather and corn in it: they also began to be very busy and troublesome to our guards; whereupon, at the next Council of War, the affair was disputed, and a resolution made for a grand sally on that part of the town, which was accordingly performed, and Sir Charles commanded in chief, marching at the head of the horse, and Sir George Lisle commanded the foot; the whole party consisted of five hundred foot, and two hundred horse, out of which, a forlorn party being drawn, they first marched down towards the river, whilst the enemy's guard was placed on both sides of the street, and a barricado across, from whence, with their chase-shot from their drakes, and small shot from the barricado and guard-houses they played very thick upon them, having no other passage over the river than a foot-bridge, the end whereof reached within five feet of the enemy's barricado but, as if it had been only a sporting skirmish amongst tame soldiers at a general muster, they regarded it not, and running in a single file over the bridge, and some for haste through the river mounted their barricado, and beat the enemy off in an instant, and having once gained that, overturned the drakes, and charged upon other parties that still fired at them in the street, and passed by the guard-houses, till they had cleared a great part of the street; surrounding them, charged in upon them, who having neither possibility of relief, retreat, or escape, yielded upon quarter; so they took the Captain, Lieutenant, Ensign and about eighty private soldiers, with all the other inferior officers.

Sir George Lisle

Many were also killed in the adjacent houses, the whole street being almost full of soldiers: they overturned the drakes, and threw one of them into the river, but not having teams ready could not bring them off. The whole party being now marched up, and having thus surprised the guard they marched on, and made good the charge till they had cleared the whole street, which gave so great an alarm to all their leaguer, that they immediately rallied together all the foot and horse on that side of the river, and marched down the hill from behind the Windmill to the top of another hill in a very full and orderly body, leaving only their colours and pikes, with a reserve behind the Windmill. But our party having gained almost the top of the first hill, followed their charge so smartly upon them, that they soon forced them to a disorderly retreat, and quickly made them strive to take leave of their ground: the fields were overspread with confused and dispersed soldiers both of horse and foot.

Our party being thereby encouraged, prosecuted their reserves till they had beat them behind the Windmill, and forced not only their reserve and colours, but all they had or could rally to quit the ground and disperse themselves; insomuch, that they were forced to divide their horse into three squadrons or bodies, one division to keep the field against ours, who had now made a stand into better order; and the other two constantly wheeled up and down, beating up their foot as they ran away: and their foot would never have disputed a hedge, had they not taken this course, which was now their refuge, and we had immediately cleared all that part of the leaguer.

But having now gotten a very thick hedge for their shelter, and being thus forced up, began to make a stand; and our foot more out of heat of courage than mature policy, having engaged thus far, some of them still ran on, till they gained an old thin hedge opposite to the enemy beyond the Windmill, where they still fired upon the enemy, maintaining the said hedge, whilst a party of the enemy's horse wheeled about the field between them; which party accidentally discovered they had spent all their ammunition, by hearing a soldier foolishly call out for some, and thereupon clapping spurs to their horse, made a full charge upon them through the hedge, which they might easily do at any part of it, who not having ammunition nor time to retreat, were most of them killed and taken prisoners; till when we had lost very few in the charge, though many were wounded, as could not otherwise be avoided in so smart an engagement: though the Saints of our times would make us believe, they have found out a way of fighting to kill thousands, with the loss of very few unites; but 'tis only tongue-charms which guard their armies, and not Devine Providence which conducts them to such miracles.

Now the body of our party being upon their retreat, and perceiving what had happened, faced about again, and received their charge with such an undaunted retort, that they forced them once more to a speedy retreat; and so marched easily into the town again, in very good order.

In this action, Sir George Lisle was once taken prisoner, but immediately rescued; and in all we lost one Captain, one Lieutenant, and about thirty private soldiers, who were taken at the broken hedge, but very few killed.

Mr. Weston, a gentleman of the General's troop being shot in the belly, was also taken prisoner.

Of the enemy's, upwards of eighty were brought into the town prisoners, and between two and three hundred killed; amongst whom was the Colonel that succeeded Colonel Needham, in the command of his regiment, who was killed the first night's attack and many of them wounded; of which very few escaped, but died within a very short time, as their party confessed themselves to our prisoners, either through neglect of their surgeons, (in which we suffered very much also within the town) or through the severity of the weather, insomuch that divers that came into the town afterwards, and these men too that had been formerly in the King's service, affirmed that the attack was at the least five hundred men loss to them; besides many that left the leaguer upon it, some coming into the town, three or four in a day, and often more, for a long time together; and others stealing away to their own habitations.

After which sally the countrymen began to be displeased with the service, and thought it hard duty to lie so long in the trenches, and were glad to entertain all comers who would perform their duty for them, allowing them ten shillings a week constant pay, to be excused themselves; by which means, many who came from London, and other places, with design to have joined us, not being able to come into the town, entered themselves in the army; though at the same time they intended to have joined us, had it been our fortunes to have marched into the field, as they declared. But Heaven had otherwise ordained it, having a farther judgment for this wretched nation.

The next night, the enemy strengthening their leaguer on that part of the town, fell into the street again, with a stronger party than before, and possessed themselves of their former guards and ground, and again fell to firing the houses, on that side of the river next the town, intending thereby to have fired our guards, which we had now placed in the face of them, being only a narrow river betwixt them, who much detrimented them, and kept the fire from doing us any harm: they then set fire to all the Windmills near the town, thinking thereby to hinder us from grinding our corn, but we soon found a salve for that fore; for, finding at the Hythe by the river side many mill-stones designed for transportation, some of them were fortunately brought into the town, when we were in possession of that place, and divers horse-mills were set up, which proved very serviceable during the Siege.

Then they raised two or three horn-works and redoubts on the north side of the leaguer, running their trench up to them from the river side over against the Warren, where they placed divers great pieces, which they played violently at a mill called the Middle-Mill upon the river, which mill they supposed was the only one we had left; and indeed it was, excepting those horse-mills; but they did little damage to the said mill, which greatly displeased them, for they thought, if they disabled us from grinding corn for the soldiers, they would mutiny for want of bread; which was probable enough, and might have happened, having such poisonous incendiaries to set them on, who had privately intruded themselves amongst them, and the town's-people were always ready to second them; but this was happily prevented, by the diligent care of the Lord Loughborow, who made a most laborious toil as pleasing to him as the lightest recreation, by undertaking and continuing the general care of providing all necessary provisions for the army, which was daily ordered and distributed by the Commissaries, to the whole town, insomuch that he would many times, half a day together, continue his strict eye over both mills and bakers, left by their indiscreet or wilful neglect, any inconveniencies should happen.

The same care was also ordered to be taken by the Mayor for the inhabitants of the town, who was commanded by the Council of War, to raise supplies of provision for the people, and to set up mills for the grinding their corn, who by this time began to be in want, the town very full of them and many of them very indigent and needy, who were not in a capacity to provide for themselves, nor had they scarcely been when the town was open: but the Mayor (whether out of a rebellious wilfulness, or sottish simplicity, I leave others to judge) rather desired to hazard the starving them, thinking, that by the violent instigation of unmerciful hunger, they would be urged to a mutiny in the town, whereby the enemy might take hold of the confusion amongst ourselves, and overwhelm us in a sudden and general destruction; for notwithstanding all threats, and daily urgencies from the Lord Loughborow and Sir Charles Lucas, he still neglected to provide corn for those who had none, or mills to grind for those who had yet some left.

Whereupon, the poor of the town, having quite exhausted their provision, began to throng together, making great clamours and exclamations of their being ill used, and falling into necessity, their bellies sounding alarms to their mouths, made their mouths instruments to thunder their wants to the ears of the Officers of the army, who did not at all reflect on the Mayor and Officers of the town: but Sir Charles Lucas, at the next Council of War, commiserating them as his own town's-born people, petitioned the Lords that they might have some corn delivered them out of the general store-house, which was as readily granted as mentioned, and an order immediately given; by which order the Commissaries were appointed to deliver to every family according to the number of people in it, a certain proportion of bread-corn, which amounted in the whole to three hundred quarters of wheat and rye; the want whereof proved so great an inconveniency to ourselves, that half that quantity would have supported us till we had obtained better conditions from the enemy than we did.

At a Council of War on the 12th of July, by a general consent, the Earl of Norwich caused the following declaration to be dispersed in the country, as also in the enemy's leaguer.

THE DECLARATION OF HIS EXCELLENCY GEORGE LORD GORING, EARL OF NORWICH, WITH THE GENTLEMEN AND FREEHOLDERS OF THE COUNTIES OF KENT AND ESSEX, IN ARMS FOR THE PROSECUTION OF THEIR GENERAL PETITION AND SOLEMN ENGAGEMENT; AS ALSO THEIR OFFER UNTO ALL SUCH OFFICERS AND SOLDIERS AS SHALL JOIN THEM.

"Could prosperity make us insolent, this overture should be the story of our present fortunes; how numerous, how unanimous, how associated, and how befriended have we been in our undertakings!   In a word, Heaven seems pleased with our proceedings, and earth conspires for our deliverance! Consider with what resolution we have acted in times of despair, and raised ourselves to the present height out of nothing!   Consider also, that we still move with the same resolution, and are yet favoured and encouraged by the same Providence who at first raised us.

In this condition, gentlemen and fellow subjects, we salute you in a temper of pure love and christianity; disengaged, I assure you, from any interest whatever, or mixture of revenge or fear.   Peace is the end we aim at, and proposed at first to accomplish our designs in a peaceable manner, if it were possible so to do.

We have compassionately considered the number of innocent souls who have been seduced by the imposture of a pretended liberty, and the many who have been brought into erroneous and unfortunate engagements by their necessities, all of whom must certainly perish, if not preserved by this now only remaining expedient:

Therefore, whatever Officer or Soldier now in arms against us, shall, on or before the 21st day of this instant July, repair unto us, or join any part of our forces, and with them enter upon action, and not proceed against us for the future, shall have his or their arrears paid unto him or them: and we do further hereby oblige ourselves to intercede to his most sacred Majesty, for an Act of Indemnity; and we do not in the least doubt but our most gracious sovereign the King, will immediately grant the same; and, for the performance hereof on our part, we tie our honors and the faith of the county; vowing withal, that we design no alteration, either in church or common wealth, but such as this present Parliament hath declared and allowed to be the duty of good christians and loyal subjects.

On the 23rd of July, the enemy drew down to the Hythe, where we had a guard placed in the church, but Captain Horsmander, the officer who then commanded the guard, no sooner saw the enemy, but he delivered up his guard of soldiers, without firing of one musquet; whereas, had he opposed them, he might in a very short time have been relieved and drawn off, though the place could not have been maintained. This place proved of very little benefit to them; for, by that time, we had scarce left any provision or ammunition there, only they might reflect on themselves for the neglect they had committed, in permitting us to keep it so long within our quarters, when, with much ease, they might have taken it from us, for it lay so open for them to have seized, that had they made an attempt upon it, we could not have kept it without engaging our whole body, and quitting the town; and indeed, had they surprised that place in due time, as they might easily enough have done before it was drained, we could not have kept possession of the town ten days, for there lay the greatest part of our provision by which we afterwards subsisted.

The next day, having drawn the line very near the Lord Lucas's house, they planted two demi-cannons against St. Mary's Church, from whence they fired upwards of sixty great shot at the steeple of St. Mary's Church, but did very little damage, for with as much expedition as possible, a battery was raised against them upon the curtain; from whence we had not fired more than four times before one of their best cannoneers fell, and with him six men more; upon which, finding that place too warm for their continuance, they removed their guns from thence.

Now the occasion of their being so envious as to aim at the destruction of that steeple, was on account of our keeping a centinel continually there, who discovered their motion both night and day; besides which, we had made a platform in the frame of the bells, and planted a brass saker there, which flanking their trench, did them much injury.

Lord George Goring

On the 25th day, the enemy drawing their line still nearer the Lord Lucas's house, under the shelter of an old wall, and some buildings, brought up the aforesaid demi-cannons, and battering upon the Gate-House (wherein was a guard of one hundred musqueteers) reduced one side of it to the ground, which falling amongst their work (being a small half moon, drawn from one side of the house to the other) annoyed them very much; the enemy also fired two or three granadoes at the same time, which buried many in the stones and dust, and the rest, not able to stand the shock, betook themselves to their swords, and the but-ends of their musquets, and fought very hard from one place to another, after losing their line, till most of them got away, some out of the wicket of the gate, and others out of the windows, and broken places of the house. The Officers also forced their liberty with the points of their swords, and came all off safe.

The enemy could not boast much of their success in this action; though it was some advantage to them; but they purchased it with the loss of many a stout man, and of their oldest soldiers, whom they quickly found lying by the wall and sides of the trench, some dead, and others speaking well of the gallant behaviour of their enemy, in their miserable dying groans. Of the whole guard, consisting of a hundred men, not above ten were taken prisoners, and only four or five killed, many I confess were wounded, but came off, and afterwards recovered.

Destruction of St. John's Abbeygate, July 1648

Having thus possessed themselves of this house, as was their customary way of proceeding in all other places, the first thing thought on was plunder and accordingly, they fell to searching the house, and those things which were moveable in it, though of little worth, or service, they took away; which chiefly consisted of bedsteads, stools, and the like, for the said house had been divers times before plundered; and I believe was one of the first in the kingdom served so: but on finding themselves no better rewarded for their service, that they might be more notorious in their villainy, they broke open the vault wherein the ancestors of the Lucas's family were usually interred, under pretence of searching for money, and finding several corpse not quite dissolved, particularly the corpse of the Lady Lucas, and the Lady Killigrew, who were buried in leaden coffins; they tore open the said coffins, dismembered their trunks, throwing a leg in one corner of the vault, and an arm in another, and were so impudent in this brutish act, as to take away the hair of those Ladies' heads in their hats, as a triumphant bravado in honor of their villainy; in this condition the vault continued till the corpse of Sir Charles Lucas, that loyal martyr was brought to be entombed there.   This was beyond what had ever been known or heard of before, among the most inhuman and barbarous monsters!   And is not that common-wealth happy which must receive a reformation from such saints, who had, for ten years before been practicing acts, absolutely monstrous even to nature itself, beyond parallel or precedent to the most subtle machavillian, or bloody tyrants in the world.

But to return; by this time, our magazine began to be pretty near empty, all our flesh being spent; whereupon, the next affair that was ordered, was the searching the private stores that were in the town; which was accordingly done, but they proved very weak.   Then the Council of War, after receiving an account of the searches, what condition the town was in, as to provision, and who had now examined every private family, ordered that all the horse, excepting two hundred, should in the night sally forth, and break through the leaguer, and if they could get through with such ease as they wished, to march northward, in hopes of relief; for at that time, we had received very great assurance, by private letters, that relief was intended, and hasting towards us from Duke Hamilton, under the command of Sir Marmaduke Langdale; so the horse were all drawn to a rendezvous in the Castle-Yard, late in the night, and a party of foot with them, for their assistance, in forcing the enemy's line, with pioneers, to level the way for them to let the horse in when the foot should have forced the enemy off their line, which was easy to have been performed; thus they marched over the river by the Middle-Mill, and came within reach of the enemy's sentinels, before they were discovered; or any part of the guards alarmed, but their guides and pioneers, who were for the most part townsmen, agreeable to a plotted combination amongst them, ran away immediately the night being dark. By which cowardly behaviour we were forced to retreat again into the town, which was done, without the loss of a man; but it gave the enemy so much notice, as to make an absolute discovery of our designs, and it was afterwards not thought proper to make a second attempt.

At the next Council of War, considering the stores were exhausted, and all flesh or very near all was spent, it was thought convenient to keep those horses which were fitting for the soldiers to eat; so they were drawn into the Castle-Yard, with orders, that not any officer whatsoever, should conceal their horses, but cause them to be brought into the field, upon the forfeiture of them to be slaughtered immediately; when the third part of every troop was drawn out and delivered to the Commissary to be killed, some of whom to be immediately distributed to the men, and the rest to be powdered; which the soldiers very willingly submitted to, and as cheerfully fed upon them, rather than deliver themselves up to their enemies, upon base or dishonorable terms; which expressions of theirs were so common and public, that the enemy hearing of our falling to horse flesh, heard also of the resolution of the soldiery, which greatly startled them; for before then, they hoped for and expected our daily submission to a treaty of surrender.

Now upon the last search which was made in the townsmens' houses and shops for all things eatable, very little corn was found, in some houses not above a peck, in some two, some none, or scarcely any flesh, yet there was a good quantity of spice and oil, which, as far as it would hold out, proved very useful to eat with the horse flesh; some starch was also found, which was preserved, and the same made very good puddings.

It hath been reported, that at this time, we had some relief brought to us by water from the fleet at sea, but it was not true, for although there was a river which came up to the town, yet the sea was upwards of seven miles from the town; and besides, the enemy had possessed themselves of the block-house against the island of Mersea, which commanded the pass into it, so that no boat could stir by them to the Hythe, which was the nearest place that they could come.

It was confidently asserted, that the ruin of our whole undertaking, was occasioned by our giving the enemy liberty of possessing themselves of Mersea Fort; but they are certainly in the wrong who think so. We at first intended to have possessed ourselves of the said fort, and Colonel Tuke was named for that expedition; but, after duly considering the situation of our affairs, we were fully convinced that the said design could not be beneficial to us, and for these very good reasons:

First, The Fort at Mersea, was upwards of seven miles distance from us, and the enemy having beset the town quite round, it was consequently in their power to stop any communication betwixt us and Mersea.

Secondly, It was reasonable to think, that as the enemy were surrounding the town, they would also take possession of the said fort, which they accordingly did, and as we could not have afterwards sent any relief to our forces there, they must have been cut in pieces, or taken prisoners.

Thirdly, In our consultation about taking Mersea Fort, and placing a guard there, we found that the said island was not capable of relieving and supporting half the body of men necessary for the defence and security of the place.

Fourthly, We did not think it policy to divide our army, and thereby much weaken it, without some hopes of doing service; whereas there could be none as affairs stood, especially as our number was not sufficient to engage at both places.

But others say, that had we taken and kept possession of Mersea Fort, we might have been relieved by the ships of war at sea, who we knew paid due submission to the Royal Authority; but relief from them was very uncertain, for we well knew it was with difficulty they could obtain provision for their men; and it ought to be considered, that five hundred men placed at the fort, would have been a sufficient number to have kept our party there till they were starved; it not being possible for us to afford them the least assistance when surrounded as aforesaid; and that by the same means, all persons were hindered from assisting or joining us.

After the enemy had obtained possession of the Lord Lucas's house, and the Hythe, they began to draw their line still more straight about us, and to lie quite round us, insomuch that we were confined within a very narrow compass: they also brought up their biggest pieces of battery, viz. Two demi-cannons, and two whole calverins, which they placed near St. John's house and again fell to battering St. Mary's steeple, one side of which was some hours after beat down, with a great part of the said church; they also broke the saker which was placed in it; during all which smart firing, not one man was killed, and only one of the matrosses wounded.

On the 25th in the night, the enemy alarmed us round the line, and fell upon our guard in the Middle-Mill, over against Rye-Gate, commanded by Colonel Rainsborow, and getting over the river at a fordable place, fell upon them furiously and obliged them to retreat into the town, afterwards set fire to the mill; upon which a party of the town, (chiefly gentlemen) marched down upon them, and attacked them with such resolution and spirit, that they were obliged to take to their legs and run away, first throwing down their arms, and their retreat was in such disorder, that many of them mistaking the proper place to get over the river at, were drowned in their passage. Twelve of the enemy were killed on the spot, and six taken prisoners; and the mill being then on fire, the soldiers present were commanded to take water in their hats and quench the same; which was accordingly done, and with such expedition, that little damage ensued.

St. Mary's at the Walls Church

This night the enemy intended to have stormed the town; but on meeting with this repulse, laid aside their designs.

The following accident happened in the attack, to an Ensign in our guard, in Colonel Till's regiment, viz. He was shot through the body, in at one side and out at the other, with a five pound bullet, after which he went from the guard to his quarters in the heart of the town, by the help of one soldier only, who led him, the bullet hanging by his side in his skin, and being laid on his bed, the bullet broke out, and carried with it, his last spirits of life; giving him time to breathe out this expression only:

"Oh! that I had been shot with my colours in my hand, that furling myself in them, I might have so died, my friends might have believed, I really loved the King, and that I lived , and cheerfully died in his and my country's service."

An expression, as gallant, as the strangeness of the shot by which he died; 'tis pity the memory of so great and loyal a gentleman, should sleep in obscurity, when he ought to be an everlasting trophy in the hearts of all true christian royalists and conscientious subjects.

The 27th day, the enemy lying in Magdalen-Street, (vulgararly called Maudlin-Street) began to cast up two or three redoubts in the field betwixt the said street and the town, over against Berry-Fields, (for so were the fields called next East-Gate) and beginning to express their intentions by their turbulent behaviour, we supposed they designed to be ill neighbours; whereupon a party was drawn out, which made a smart sally upon them, and beat them off from their works, and followed them into the streets and houses, and killed many of them, still maintaining their ground although it were noon-day, till the enemy began to draw great bodies of horse and foot upon them, when they made an orderly and fair retreat, bringing off ten or more prisoners, with the loss of one man and two wounded; after their growing thus near us, daily sallies were made in one place of their leaguer or other, till the end of the Siege.

On the Sunday following Sir William Massam, one of the committee, who was then prisoner in the town, was sent forth in exchange for Mr. Ashburnham, whose man was permitted to come to the walls, where he received him; and he was joyful enough of his liberty from that imprisonment though some boldly aspersed the gentleman under whom the Committee-men were prisoners, and declared that they were placed just upon line, because they should be killed by the impartial shot of their friends; which is false, for they were lodged at our first coming to town, at the best and most convenient inn, and afterwards the town being very full, would not admit any better conveniency for them, and I am sure, if they will acknowledge only the truth, they must confess, civility enough was showed them to the end, being allowed to receive any provisions of fresh and hot meats, as venison pasties, and the like, into the town, without the least opposition or affront, whilst the lords and gentlemen themselves, fed generally on horse flesh. I confess that once or twice, the top of the house wherein they were confined, was shot through with great shot from the leaguer, whereupon they sent a special message to the Lord Fairfax, to let him know what house they lay in, and desired him that he would not shoot that way; but this was very empty, for what house in the town could be secure from the fire? They should have gotten an order of parliament that the bullets should not have dared to molest them, if they did fly that way.

Royalist gunner on top of St. Mary's Church Tower

The enemy proceeding thus in their Siege, in a very formal order, crept with their approaches nearer and nearer to us; yet many of their men paid dearly for their boldness, and though by reason of the scarcity of our ammunition, we could not make very great sallies upon them, nor constantly fire from the line, yet sallies were made almost every day, in one part or other, and our shot so carefully disposed of, that many of them fell daily; some of our men they often killed when going out to cut and bring in grass for the horse; for we had no horse meat left in the town, but what they first fought for and brought in and sold; going in parties, and some firing at the enemy whilst the others cut grass, all the thatch from the houses, and boughs from the trees, being eat up; setting those aside, we lost but few men during the Siege.

On the 10th of August, the Lady Katharine Scot, accompanied with some other ladies desired leave of the Lord Fairfax, that she might have the liberty of going to the Lord Norwich, her father, (the Lady Norwich being newly dead) but could not procure so much favour as to go into the town to him, but only to come to the Sally-Port to which, she was accompanied with a guard, who might hear all the discourse that should pass betwixt them; there came with them the Quartermaster General Gravener, and some other officers, and were entertained with a collation of horse flesh and a bottle or two of wine, the best accommodation we could treat them with, which they ate heartily on and liked.

And now began horse flesh to be as precious to us as the choicest meats before, the soldiers in general, and all officers and gentlemen, from the lords to the lowest degree or quality eating nothing else, unless cats and dogs, which the enemy disgusted very much, daily expecting us to surrender; by the assurance whereof, they constantly encouraged their soldiers to the continuance of the hard duty they then underwent, who else would have been hardly kept together, being often upon the march, either away into the country, or else to join us in the town.

It was by this time grown so delicious a food amongst the soldiers, that we could scarcely secure our horses in the stables, for every morning one stable or other was robbed, and our horses knocked on the head and sold in the shambles by the pound; nor was there in a short time a dog left, for it was customary for each soldier to reserve half his ammunition loaf, and in a morning walk the streets, and if he discovered a dog, to drop a piece of bread, and so decoy him on till within his reach, and then with the but-end of his musquet knock his brains out, and march away with him to his quarters. I have known six shillings given for the side of a dog, and yet but a small one neither.

Now the enemy perceiving they could not work upon us by summons, threats, nor force of arms, had recourse to petty stratagems, sometimes sending false fire of strange improbable news of great victories over the Scots, long before they ever received them; and lists of prisoners who were taken never in arms, and such like whimsies, hoping thereby to terrify the inferior fort of soldiers, and bring them to a timorous apprehension of their condition, and who might probably force their officers by their mutinous resolutions to treat for conditions, to leave them in the lurch, which latter of the two, the enemy rather wished that so many gentlemen might fall a prey to their unsatiable malice.

They also sent private papers into the town amongst the soldiers by women, incensing the soldiers against their officers, reproaching them with that odious name of rebels, (which they knew more properly belonged to themselves) and men acting against the peace of the kingdom without proper commission, all which they hoped, would so poison the brains of the soldiers, that if they would not mutiny, yet at least the greatest part would be incensed against their officers and quit the line, by whose loss we should have been so weakened, as to have been easily stormed and taken.

But instead of receiving any benefit by these suckling stratagems, they wrought nothing more than an injury to themselves; for it engaged the soldiers to higher resolutions.

Then they shot arrows into the town at several places with papers fastened to them, promising our soldiers, that if they would desert the town, they should have fair quarters, pardon for what they had done, and liberty to go to their own homes, with passes from the General, without being plundered or suffering the least prejudice or injury; but this neither proved any benefit to them or injury to us, but still rather exasperated and enlivened the soldiers who were so courageous in their resolutions as very often to express, that they would either live with liberty, or die with honor, neither of which could arise by a poor submission of an ignoble enemy.

And now the enemy had possessed themselves of all places of conveniency and advantage round about the town, and began to annoy us very much in divers places about the line, from the opposite and flanking houses, and our magazines began to grow very low of powder, so that an order was given out that the soldiers should be careful not to waste their ammunition by firing without a real occasion, and that no gunner should fire a cannon without the command of a Field Officer of his post, or a General Officer of the field. But these houses under the line proved so obnoxious, that by degrees they made that line almost too hot for any to abide it; and the enemy having found this advantage, drew thicker down upon the suburbs, under the shelter of the houses, which the officers being sensible of, and knowing there remained no securer remedy, sallied out amongst them, and beat them out of the streets, and some houses they set fire to, having first given order to those inhabitants who remained in them to secure and convey away their goods first; and those which lay immediately under the line and wall, they first pulled down by carpenters and other workmen, that the materials might be preserved, and the less prejudice done to the town and owners; which should they have let stand, would have proved so miserable an inconveniency, that we could not have maintained the town half an hour; I am confident, had the enemy ever attempted a resolute storm when once they had beset us so close; by reason that in many places the stairs came up to the top of the wall in the highest places of it, so large that two or three men might have come up a-breast, and some rooms equalled the height of the wall in a perfect diameter. And if the enemy had taken no other benefit but the opportunity of a wind and set fire to them, they might probably have set fire to the whole town; which they attempted the first night, and once afterwards had effected, had not the wind been very calm, and the soldiers extraordinary diligent in quenching the flames as fast as they fired.

On the 11th day, more arrows were again shot into the town, to entice the soldiers with alluring charms, intermixed with severe threats to quit the service; intimating, that if they came not away before the next Monday, (it being then Friday) that not a man which came after should have any quarter; which messages the soldiers still resented so much, that they resolved to answer it by the same messengers, and took some of their own arrows, anointing them with a t—d, and wrapping the same in paper, fastened it to the heads of the arrows, and writ on the paper this superscription, "An answer from Colchester, August the 11th, 1648, as you may smell," Intimating thereby how little they regarded their baits or esteemed their threatenings.

By this time, the greatest part of our horse had changed their stables for slaughter-houses, and their riders being willingly dismounted, took up with foot arms, the gentlemen halberts, and the private troopers scythes, ready fitted with long staves for the service, which were very terrible for execution; and there were many scythes found in the town upon a search for arms; more than ever was known to be in the town before; and many brown bills were also made in the town; so that no man need be idle for want of arms; these men were all enlisted, both gentlemen and private troopers (for more orderly disposing them to duty and service) in particular companies, under the Lord General, the Lord Capell, and Sir Charles Lucas; the Lord Capell marching himself on foot, with a halbert on his shoulder in the head of his company to the guard, that none might make any scruple or be dissatisfied with it; which company lay constantly upon reserve, in tents built purposely for them; which point of war must of necessity arise from as high a conveniency as any, and indeed was a course constantly practiced amongst the best and most judicious conquerors of the world, and they have left us arguments for it's support in the Chronology of divers victories obtained, and lost fields recovered by fortunate and resolute reserves, although but of small numbers, of which I shall instance one of Serverus the Emperor, who in a battle against Albinus, General of the Britons before Lugdenhum, was himself put to flight, beaten off his horse and hid himself, whilst the Britons followed the chase, chanting out their praise as victors; till Laetus, one of Serverus's officers, staying behind with some fresh troops, and making a fresh charge, the Serverians took heart again, and mounting Serverus, put on his purple fur coat, (a military mantle,) when the Albenians thinking themselves masters of the field, being disordered and

Lord Arthur Capel

furiously charged by fresh troops, after a short resistance fled, the Serverians following them to the city gates, and did vast execution.

Now these companies must not be understood for the only reserves we had, for it was the constant method of duty in the army in general, to lie every regiment on their several posts, the one half upon guard, and the other all night very near at the most convenient places upon reserve.

Thus we maintained and held out the town, in defiance of a proud, successful and imperious enemy, (this being the 17th day of August) still cherishing our hopes of relief, having yet no certain intelligence of the state of affairs in the other parts of the kingdom, nor relief approaching, and our stores were very much wasted, insomuch that our corn was very near spent, and little ammunition left to maintain only our guards with.

Therefore, at a general Council of War, his excellency the Lord Norwich, the Lord Capell, and Sir Charles Lucas, signed letters to the Lord Fairfax, desiring him to grant them twenty days respite and a pass through their quarters, for some gentlemen whom they would send to Sir Marmaduke Langdale, in order to receive a real information of his condition; and that if they found him as the enemy had given out, and nothing advancing towards us, and that there were no hopes of redress from any other quarters, that they would then treat for surrender.

Now no other hopes we had left (and indeed but little reason for these) the Duke of Buckingham and the Earl of Holland's parties were already reduced to nothing; indeed without doing any real service, and no other parties had risen; or had expressed any inclinations, much less intentions so to do.

But this request they would not grant; upon which, we were forced to send away private spies and messengers, and concluded in a general resolution, to maintain and defend the town to the last; and not to be idle with the enemy, but as active as the want of ammunition would admit; according to which resolutions, we sent out a party every day or night to the Sally-Port; and who went upon duty with great willingness, and sallying upon them, were very troublesome to them, and kept them upon constant and hard duty; but *ultra posse, non eft effe*; and our ammunition was so exhausted, that we could not send out great parties often, yet found out a way, with what materials could be gotten, to make some match; which, though it were not so good as what we had before, yet served our present necessity, and some powder also we made, but it was not much, for we were forced to resign, before we could bring it to perfection.

Then our Commissaries began to complain that their stores were almost empty; the people generally much necessitated for want of bread (the true staff of life) and the poorer sort, merely for want of corn, were ready to starve, we not being able to relieve them.

Then the poor people of the town, petitioned the Lord Fairfax, by the Mayor and Aldermen, that they might have liberty to leave the town and disperse themselves into the country, amongst their friends, who they pretended would keep them from famishing: but he did not think proper to grant them their requests, and on the contrary gave order to his whole army round the leaguer, that if any should be turned out by us, they should fire at them; at which time, they were told by their bosom friends in the town, and who were our inveterate enemies, that we had made proclamation that whoever had not twenty days provision in their houses should depart the town, as well rich as poor; at which time search being again made, few were found to have provision for more than two or three days, and the enemy having given this unchristian-like, though political order, it would have been a very ungenerous act, to have forced so many people through a sally-port; besides which, the attempt was dangerous, for they were just ready to mutiny, and would certainly have done so directly, had we forced them from their own houses upon the swords of a most cruel and merciless enemy.

Then the stores were again reviewed, and the magazines also, and the stores found to be so empty as not to yield two or three days provision of bread for the whole army, and the magazine not to maintain two hours fight if a storm should happen.

Upon which, a Council of War was again summoned, and it was agreed, that it was the best course to treat with the enemy in time; which motion being carried by a majority of voices, letters were accordingly drawn up, and Dr. Glyston a physician, then living in the town employed in the message.

And now we had done our utmost, and had proceeded as far as possible for men in our condition, having engaged a potent and conquering enemy a long time with an inconsiderable party, and were at last destitute of any relief in so short a time as our conditions would enable us to hold out.

The next morning, the Doctor returned from the enemy, bringing this answer from the General.

"That as we had held out so long against him, and to the utmost denied his summons, the best conditions we must expect from him, must be to submit to mercy; for that only the inferior officers and soldiers should have liberty to go to their own homes."

This answer displeased us much, and we were resolved not to surrender on those dishonorable conditions.

On Tuesday the 22nd, early in the morning, more arrows were shot into the town at several places of the line, with papers fastened to them, wherein was written as followeth:

August 21, 1648.

"WHEREAS on Sunday last, in a letter to Lord Goring, Lord Capell, and Sir Charles Lucas, conditions were offered to all private soldiers and inferior officers under captains, to have leave to go to their own homes without injury or violence; and all superior officers, lords and gentlemen to submit to mercy; and whereas the same hath been concealed from the soldiers and inferior officers aforesaid; nevertheless, if they will before Thursday next, lay hold on the said conditions, and come away in a body from the enemy, the same conditions shall be performed to them which have been offered; but in case they shall suffer the town's people (whom we will not receive) to be turned out of the town, and suffer the to perish under the walls, they must expect no mercy; and if the townsmen who were in arms should join with the soldiery in coming forth in a body as aforesaid, they should also be free from violence."

This mean stratagem, they thought, would have infused such a wild-fire in the mutinous brains of the lower rank of people, as would in an instant blow our interest into air, and invited the soldiery to have delivered their officers up as a sacrifice to obtain their own liberty; but their hopes were also disappointed in this; for, instead of a complacent acceptance of these propositions, they resolved to accept of no conditions wherein their officers should not receive the same benefit as themselves.

The Council of War having also the day before permitted Dr. Glyston to go out again, and Mr. Sheffield (one of the committee-men, who was then prisoner in the town, brought by us from Chelmsford) to mediate with the General for the people of the town, sent also by him other letters concerning the soldiery for conditions of surrender, but the following answer was returned.

"That they had given us a former account of what conditions they would give us, and those they would stand to, and no other must we expect."

And now we were drawn to a sad exigency, and plunged into very great extremities, and it was not for us to prolong time, but rather add wings to our resolutions, and close up our misfortunes as well as we could with an honorable conclusion, and with the best condition and greatest expedition that could be. We had scarce left uneaten one cat or dog in the town, some horses we had yet alive, but not many, for there were at that time in the Commissary's accompt a list of seven hundred and thirty horses which had been killed by him, and orderly distributed out; besides those that the soldiers had stolen out of the stables and killed, and others that gentlemen had slaughtered for their own private tables, which, I am confident, made the number above eight hundred; and as for bread, there was not corn left for one day's provision, and there were many mouths to feed, and we had made all kind of corn the town would afford, as malt, barley, oats, wheat, rye, peafe, and all we could recover into bread, for eight weeks together to lengthen our store, still contented to undergo any hardship that might probably tend to the advancement of the general good; but our hopes were now quite dissolved into absolute fear, of unavoidable ruin.

Yet this ghastly appearance of our interest, could not exile that incomparable courage which generally inspired this gallant party with lively actions and patient sufferings, as if it had been equally indifferent to them, contentedly to undergo prosperity or misfortunes; all mens' resolutions were set on fire to desperate designs, and by some unprecedented attempt, desirous of ruining their enemy, or to perish nobly in the enterprise; since it is much better to die honorably than live bafely.

The meanest of the soldiers as yet, held a conformable obedience to the commands of their officers, were undaunted in their courage, and courageous in their actions, notwithstanding the many designs and political engines the enemy had employed to alienate them from their duty, and dishearten them in their service.

But lest there might be any misunderstanding betwixt the soldiers and their officers, upon putting any design in execution, the following engagement was drawn up and signed by all the officers and gentlemen through the quarters.

"We whose names are hereunto written, do, in the presence of Almighty God, protest against all conditions, which are or shall be sent from the enemy, by which our liberties may be infringed, and our honors blemished. And we do upon our honors, solemnly engage ourselves not to desert one another, nor the foot soldiers, till by God's assistance, we have forced our passage through all that shall oppose us, or perish in the act, which we attest this 23rd of August, 1648."

Then the town was again searched, in order to find what provisions were left, and a severe account was given; all private stores were taken and brought to the Commissaries, leaving to every family who had most one peck of corn, of all or any sorts, yet after all, the whole would scarce amount to one day's provision of bread.

The next day (being Thursday the 24th) the enemy sent a paper kite into the town, which hovering a good while over it, that the soldiers might take notice thereof, at last they let it drop into the midst of the town, with many papers fixed to it, to the same purpose as those before shot in with the arrows, and with them a book, containing, "The Relation of a great Victory over the Scots, and their general Rout:" Within two hours after which, they made a general triumph through the whole leaguer, giving a volley both of small and great shot round the town in all quarters, and some of the shot playing thick into the town, gave us a very strong alarm, and as great hopes that it was either the fore-runner of a storm, or the beginning of one, till perceiving it at so great a distance as beyond and about the Windmill, below the East-Street: at the same time their assurances were so strong of gaining a victory without blows, that they thought (as indeed they had reason so to do) it would be best policy to forbear, although they had drawn their approaches so near the line under Berry-Fields by the shelter of a wall, which is yet standing, that their soldiers from the trenches and ours from the line, might talk together, and throw stones at one another, both which they frequently did.

On Friday the 25th, the Council of War met again early in the morning, at which they resolved to send General Fairfax the following letter into the leaguer.

"That since he denied to treat upon any conditions that were honorable, notwithstanding our actions and demeanors in the service, had been nothing but what became our honor and fidelity, if he were pleased to make an attempt of attacking us, he should not need to spring any mine, as he boasted they had already done; but that any gate about the town that he should make choice of, should be set open, and his entrance disputed afterwards."

But he thought himself sure of having us at an easier rate than the loss of so much blood, which a surprise of such a sort must have cost him, had he carried it, which he would hardly have done; and indeed it was his best policy not to storm us at all, since he had leisure enough to wait for our destruction, the kingdom in general being so dull and sluggish, as not to act any thing which might require his removal; which if he had done, by rising in any part thereof, though in small parties only, at that time they might have forced him either to have attempted a surprise by storm, or fairly retreated with the hazard of his honor, if not his army; for, had he stormed us, we had endangered the shattering of his whole body, the edge of whose fury was by this time taken off, and where frightened at our scythes and scalding pitch, which was kept boiling in iron pots and caldrons every night round the line, with long ladles to cast it over the rampart upon them, had they began their storming.

Whereupon, considering the melancholy condition we were plunged into, through the defeat of the Scots, the disloyalty of the whole kingdom, and the want we were of provision to subsist withal, not having any hopes of holding out two days longer, unless without bread, which we must do, or not at all; it was the final resolution of the Council of War, to draw out the whole party that night to their arms, both horse and foot, with what ammunition was left, which was not much; and as many short scaling ladders procured in the interim; and in the deadest time, when we might be least expected, to set open two of the gates, and march out and storm their line, and so falling into their head quarters, beat up their whole army and relieve ourselves, or force our march through all opposition which they should endeavour to throw in our way, or perish in the attempt; and that if the private soldiers should entertain any suspicion that the gentlemen and officers who had yet horses, should seek for their own safety by flight, and leave them engaged, every man (excepting only the General and the Major-General) to pistol his own horse at the head of them; which design being agreed on, and secrecy enjoined, and every one receiving his orders according to his duty in the undertaking, the Council broke up, and every man betook himself, with the utmost of his endeavours, to the making preparation in the day-time, for the intended expedition at night.

The enemy had this day planted four great pieces of battering cannon against Berry-Fields, and fired about one hundred and forty great shot in the forenoon, against the old wall, but did very little hurt, only beat off the tops of two old ruined towers upon it, and killed three of our men.

This was taken as a fit alarm for calling the soldiers in general to the line, where they might unexpectedly be in a readiness for the intended sally at night, without bag or baggage, which was concluded generally to be left behind; knowing that, if we gained our hoped for victory we should command them again, and our enemies to boot; and that if we failed, of a certainty we should have no need of them.

This, I confess, would have been a desperate enterprise, but must be deemed noble, and had it proceeded to action, it might in all probability have been attended with honorable success, and a glorious victory; and thereby turned not only to our liberty, but the freedom and peace of the whole kingdom; as it happened once in Paris, when the Duke of Burbon being besieged, and so distressed, that his soldiers called out to him to yield rather than starve, made a resolute sally upon the French Army, destroyed the whole body, and took the

The Siege House, Colchester

King prisoner; and from thence marched against Rome, where, although he was killed, yet the army took the city, and besieged the Pope in the Castle of Angelo.

All things were got in readiness before night came on, and the ammunition and scaling ladders were brought to a particular place, ready to be carried to the line; but some time before night, there were some officers, who (although I am charitable enough to think they would not dissent from the design) alleged many arguments, that it would certainly be better to defer it till the next night, because, they pretended, that they should then be in a far better condition for the work; at whose intercession it was put off.

And that night, by a most desperate misfortune, (though by what means it happened I know not) some mutinous spirit had insinuated into the private soldiers, that the officers and the rest of the gentlemen, were resolved the ensuing night, or very suddenly, to break away through the leaguer, and escape, and leave them all engaged, to shift for themselves.

Which spark rose to such a flame, as proved a presaging comet to our succeeding ruin, and those soldiers so remarkably gallant before, gave a curb to that courageous spirit that guided their actions in an honorable obedience; and poisoning their disturbed brains, hurried them into a frenzy of desperate mutiny round the line; in some parts, they threatened to cast their officers over the line; so high was the mutiny grown before day-light, that it was rather likely to end in immediate ruin of themselves and officers too, than a pacification; for the enemy never wanted their incendiaries amongst us, to aggravate and encourage any mischief which might post forward our destruction, and who we might be assured would not only add fire to this unnatural contention, but give the enemy notice thereof, that they might make the best use of it. The lords who were concerned in the engagement, with Sir Charles Lucas, Sir William Compton, and Sir George Lisle, showed themselves; and which they actually did in all proceedings, men as active as honorable, and beyond expression in both; but never more than in the managing of this unhappy business, the rest of the officers also bestirring themselves as diligent as could be expected, and indeed to admiration, so that at length, they had wrought some mildness amongst them, by endeavouring to give them all desirable satisfaction in this their misapprehension. Yet, notwithstanding all endeavours to pacify and allay this monstrous conjured devil it proceeded on till many left their guards, and assembled in crowds about the line, and at last, whilst the Council of War was sitting, selected from among themselves about thirty persons, whom they sent to the Council, demanding to know what their intentions were, saying,

"That if they would not make and offer conditions for them, and such as they should like of, they would article for themselves over the line, and leave their officers to shift for themselves, as they understood their officers would have done by them."

This put the Council of War into great disorder and confusion, the soldiers till then, never having acted any thing dishonorable, or unlike the most gallant fellows that ever defended the town; and in my opinion, had suffered the greatest inconveniencies that ever men did, with an extraordinary cheerfulness, never showing the least discontent at any orders which were given.

The thirty persons aforesaid coming to the house where the Council sat, sent in two men, whom they supposed to be able speakers, and who being called up, the Lord Norwich assured them of the falsity of their allegation; to confirm which he also gave them a true account and understanding of the design.

After which, his Lordship made the following declaration:

"That, the Lords and Gentlemen concerned in the engagement, were so far from deserting the common soldiers, or seeking for or desiring any benefit or advantage which should be confined to themselves only, exclusive of the said soldiers, that on the contrary, they were fully resolved to become a prey, and submit to the mercy of their enemies; nay, throw themselves into the greatest inconveniencies and hardships which the cruelty of a bloody and merciless enemy could oppress them with, sooner than not free the inferior soldiery from suffering; and that it was their sincere desires to deliver themselves up prisoners to the enemy, if thereby they could purchase them an honorable liberty; for which purpose, commissioned gentlemen, were now treating with the Lord Fairfax.

To which declaration, the soldiers returned this answer, "That they desired not any liberty which should be purchased at so dear a rate," with many affectionate expressions of their resolutions to serve their officers again, not only at the present time, but at any other, when they should be commanded, and then departed very much satisfied.

This for the present, appeased the mutiny, and they were well satisfied and began to examine how this jealousy arose, but it was now unseasonable, and much too late to think of any thing but the worst of adverse fortune for their superiors, instead of present delivery; for the enemy, by their unruly behaviour knew as much of our condition in every respect, as we ourselves.

However, the soldiers were pacified and dismissed to their posts, and it was resolved, as most convenient in our condition, to send a gentlemen from the Council then sitting, to treat with the enemy for conditions, being frustrated of all hopes of longer subsistence or security, or a possibility of attempting any further design.

About this time, the Lord Fairfax offered the Lord Capell's son in exchange for one of the Committee-men, who was a prisoner in the town; but the loyal gentlemen refused it; and the Lord Capell in particular wrote word to General Fairfax, that it was inhuman to surprise his son, who was not in arms, and afterwards offer him to insult the affection of a father; however, he might murder his son if he thought proper so to do, and he would leave his blood to be revenged as Heaven should think fit; adding, that as the King's subjects had through their means been reduced to feed upon horse flesh, the prisoners in their custody, should for the future, also be accommodated with the same sort of diet.

The enemy complained that the Royalists shot poisoned bullets amongst them, and sent two affidavits, which had been made by two deserters who swore that it was done by the direction of the Lord Norwich; but the officers in the town replied under all their hands, that they disowned the practice, and never gave any such orders; that the deserters were perjured in running from their colours, and therefore not to be regarded, having fired rough-cast bullets only, and which could not be avoided in their condition.

After this, Colonel Samuel Tuke (complete in honor and integrity) was dispatched from them, with full power to accept of any conditions he could obtain, and to conclude before he came back, who returned not till very late that night, yet time enough to let us know the sad conclusion we were like to have. For General Fairfax, (at the instigation of his Council of War) was fallen from those conditions which formerly he had offered, and now they began to insult over our miseries, and the best that could be obtained, were to deliver ourselves up, the soldiers, prisoners at war, with all officers under captains and gentlemen, to submit to mercy; and that we should release the Committee-men, who were prisoners with us the next morning, if we expected any favour from him.

See a just judgment for the disobedience of the soldiers, and which they brought upon themselves, by their tumultuous and mutinous proceedings, which not only proved ruinous to many of them, but destruction to their officers, and for ought I know the ruin of a design, which might otherwise have been so prosperous, as to have given redemption to the whole kingdom from that vassallage it was unhappily plunged into.

The next morning, being Sunday the 27th of August, the Council of War met again, and this account being given in, there was no refuge, nor remedy left, nor any thing to trust to, but what conditions the enemy would give us; the Committee was therefore immediately dispatched, and Colonel Tuke, with five other officers, sent out again to the enemy, to confirm and sign articles for surrender, and the manner of delivery.

The soldiers of the enemy's army and ours were already mixed on many places of the line, and no fire given on either side, as if we had been absolute prisoners, long before any conclusion was made. Towards night they came back, and brought with them the following articles, which were to be put in execution the next morning.

ARTICLES AGREED ON THE 27th OF AUGUST, 1648. BY AND BETWEEN THE COMMISSIONERS OF HIS EXCELLENCY THE LORD GENERAL FAIRFAX, ON THEIR PART; AND THE COMMISSIONERS OF THE EARL OF NORWICH, THE LORD CAPELL, AND SIR CHARLES LUCAS, ON THE OTHER PART; FOR AND CONCERNING THE SURRENDER OF THE TOWN AND GARRISON OF COLCHESTER.

I.

That all the horses belonging to the officers, soldiers and gentlemen, engaged at Colchester, with saddles and bridles to them, shall be brought into

A
DECLARATION,

Of the Besieged Soldiers in the City of *Colchester*, and their resolution concerning the surrendring of the said City.

Also the planting two demi-Canon against it, and the battering down part of Saint Maries Church.

And how a Partie of the Lord Cepel's Shavers issued forth ef Buttolphs-gate, aud set upon our Pioneers, and tooke some prisoners, and hewed one of our men to peeces with their Sythes.

Moreover the taking of divers horse from underneath the Walls, and the killing of one of their Commanders.

Together with a true Relation of the proceedings betwixt the Scots and Major Generall Lambert, and the last news from Portsmouth.

L O N D O N Printed,
Ao. Dom. 1648.

St. Mary's Church-Yard, by nine o'clock to-morrow morning, and the spare saddles and bridles into the church, and delivered without wilful spoil, to such as the Lord General shall appoint to take charge of them.

II. That all the arms, colours and drums, belonging to any persons in Colchester above mentioned, should be brought into St. James's Church, by ten o'clock to-morrow morning, and delivered without wilful spoil or embezzlement, to such as the Lord General shall appoint to take charge of them.

III. That all private soldiers and officers under captains, shall be drawn together into the Fryar's Yard adjoining East-Gate, by ten o'clock to-morrow morning, with their cloaths and baggage; their persons to surrender into the custody of such as the said General shall appoint to take charge of them, and that they shall have fair quarters, according to the explanation, made in the answers to the first query of the Commissioners from Colchester which is hereunto annexed.

IV. That the Lords, and all Captains, and superior Officers, and Gentlemen of distinction, engaged at Colchester, shall be drawn together to the King's Head, with their cloaths and baggage, by eleven o'clock to-morrow morning, and there submit themselves to the mercy of the Lord General into the hands of such as he shall appoint to take charge of them; and that a list of the names of all the General Officers, and Field Officers, now in command in the town, be sent out to the Lord General, by nine o'clock in the morning.

V. That all the guards within the town of Colchester, shall be withdrawn from the line, forts and other places, by eight o'clock to-morrow morning, and such as the Lord General shall appoint, shall come in their room.

VI. That all the ammunition shall be preserved in the places where it lies, to be delivered to the comptroller of his excellency's train, by ten o'clock to-morrow morning; and all the wagons belonging to the soldiery, or persons engaged, with the harness belonging thereunto, shall be brought to some convenient place near the ammunition, to be delivered to the same person, at the same hour.

VII. That such as are sick and wounded in the town, shall be there kept and provided for; with accommodations requisite for men in their condition and not be removed thence, until they be recovered, or able without prejudice to their health's to remove, and shall have such chirurgeons allowed them as are in town.

VIII. That the ordnance in the town, with their appurtenances, shall without wilful spoil, be left at the several platforms and places, where they are now planted, and to be delivered to his excellency's guard, that shall take care of those places respectively.

IX. That from henceforth there shall be a cessation of arms, on both parts; but the forces within the town to keep to their own guards, and the Lord General to keep theirs, until they shall be removed according to the foregoing articles.

SIGNED BY US,

THE COMMISSIONERS ON BEHALF OF HIS EXCELLENCY THE LORD FAIRFAX.

Thomas Honeywood, Bram Gurdon, Henry Ireton, J. Sparrow, Thomas Rainsborow, Isaac Ewer,

Edward Whaley, Thomas Cook, William Bloys, G. Barnadiston.

THE COMMISSIONERS ON BEHALF OF THE EARL OF NORWICH, THE LORD CAPELL AND SIR CHARLES LUCAS.

William Compton, Abraham Shipman, Edward Hammond,

Samuel Tuke, William Ayloffe,

Hythe, August 27, 1648.

QUERIES PROPOUNDED BY THE COMMISSIONERS FROM COLCHESTER, TO THE COMMISSIONERS OF HIS EXCELLENCY THE LORD FAIRFAX, UPON THE FOLLOWING CONDITIONS.

I. **W**HAT is meant by fair quarter?

II. What is meant by rendering mercy?

To the First,

By fair quarter we understand, that with fair quarter, for their lives, they shall be free from wounding or beating, shall enjoy warm cloaths to cover them, and keep them warm, shall be maintained with victuals fit for prisoners, whilst they shall be kept prisoners.

To the Second,

By rendering mercy, we understand, that they shall be rendered, or render themselves to the said General, or whom he shall appoint, without certain assurance of quarter, so as the Lord General, may be free, to put some immediately to the sword, (if he see cause) although his excellency intends chiefly, and for the generality of those under that condition, to surrender them to the mercy of the Parliament and General. There hath been large experience, neither hath his excellency given cause to doubt of his civility, to such as he shall retain prisoners; although by their being rendered to mercy, he stands not engaged thereby.

Upon return to these answers the Commissioners from Colchester, propounded these two further queries.

I.

WHETHER those that were surrendered to mercy, shall enjoy their wearing cloaths, as well as those on their backs, as what other charge they have ?

II. Whether the Noblemen and Officers, shall have use of their own horses, to the places where they shall be confined?

To which was answered, by his Excellency's Commissioner:

TO THE FIRST,

It is intended, that those who shall be rendered and received to mercy, shall enjoy the wearing cloaths on their backs; but for more, the general will not be engaged.

TO THE SECOND,

It is expected (in case of surrender upon treaty) that all horses, as well as arms, be delivered up; and for circumstances thereof, there is to be an article yet for the gentlemen and officers under this condition in question, (when any of them shall be removed to the places of confinement) his excellency will take care for horses to carry them, with respect to their qualities; but for allowing their own horses, he will not be engaged.

A List of PRISONERS taken at the Surrender of COLCHESTER, the 28th of August, 1648.

THE Earl of Norwich,
    Colonel Lord CAPELL
Lord LOUGHBOROW
Sir CHARLES LUCAS, Col.
Sir Wm. COMPTON, Col.
Sir GEORGE LISLE, Captain
    of Foot
Sir BARNARD GASQUOIN

Sir Ric. MAULYVERER,
    escaped, and afterwards taken
Quarter–Master General
CARTER
Colonel GILBOURNE
Colonel FARRE, escaped, and
    afterwards taken.
Colonel HAMMOND

Sir ABRAHAM SHIPMAN

Sir JOHN WATTS

Sir LODOWICK DYER

Sir HENRY APPLETON

Sir DENNARD STRUT

Sir HUGH ORILEY

Colonel CHESTER

Colonel TILL

Colonel HEATH

Colonel TUKE

Colonel AYLOFFE

Colonel SAWYER

LIEUTENANT COLONELS.

CULPEPPER

LANCASTER

GOUGH

POWELL

ASHTON

BAGLEY

WISEMAN

SMITH

MAJORS.

AESCOTT

SMITH

ARMSTRONG

WARD

BAYLEY

NEALE

SCARROW

BLYNCOT

GLENNINGS

CAPTAINS

WICKS

PITS

BULLY

BURDGE

BARTROPE

LYNSEY

Lieutenant GORING

WARD

BUSBEY

PAIN

HEMOR

SMITH

MYLDMAY	KENINGTON
OSBALDISTON	HEATH
ESTWICK	NEWTON
LOVELL	BAYLEY
COOPER	STEPHENS
BLUNT	LODGE
SNELLGRAVE	LYNN
DYNORS	Lieutenant WHITE
DUFFEN	

EDWARD GOODYEARE, Master General

Commissary-General TROULEY

FRANCIS LOVELESS, Master of the Ordnance

Wagon-Master General GRAVISTON

SERVANTS attending the LORDS
and GENTLEMEN 65
LIEUTENANTS. 72
ENSIGNS and CORNETS 69
SERGEANTS. 183
PRIVATE SOLDIERS . . . . <u>3067</u>

<u>Total 3530</u>

At our surrender, there was but one barrel and a half of powder left; many great shot remained in the Lord Capell's quarters, which the enemy had fired into the town, and the soldiers gathering up, sold to him for sixpence a bullet.

Our Articles of Surrender were no sooner signed, but many of our horses were taken forcibly out of the stables by the soldiers of the leaguer, who flocked into the town before the gates were opened, contrary to the articles, and plundered everything they could lay their hands on.

And now began the last scene of this tragedy; the Lords and Gentlemen, according to the articles, met at the King's Head, and the rest of the army at their appointed places, and all things were ordered according to the conditions; and about two of the clock in the afternoon, the Lord Fairfax entered the town, and rid round to view our line and show himself in triumph to the inferior soldiers, but came not near the Lords; on surveying the town, he found a just cause for admiration, and wondered how it was possible we could maintain it so long against him, whose very name, as he thought, was enough to conquer.

He then went to his quarters in the town, where the Council of War immediately met, according to his appointment, to luxuriate their insatiable malice, in a collation of loyal blood, and thereby raise their trophies in the ruin of incomparable virtue.

And after they had insulted upon our conditions and sported away some votes of contempt upon us, we then lying at their mercy, they concluded their

The King's Head Assembly room where the Royalist officers congregated following the surrender of the town.

malicious design, and decreed a barbarous sacrifice of innocent virtue.

They sent Colonel Ewers to the King's Head, to visit, as we thought, the Lords and Gentlemen, but he brought a sentence of death in his heart, though not immediately in his mouth, which easily discovered itself in his death-like countenance; and coming up into the chamber first saluted the Lords, and afterwards came to Sir Charles Lucas, and with a flighting gesture told him that the general desired to speak to him at the Council of War, with Sir George Lisle, Sir Bernard Gasquoine and Colonel Farre, if they were there, but he was not there; upon which Sir Charles Lucas, as presaging what indeed afterwards followed, took his solemn leave of the Lords and the rest of his fellow prisoners, who were near him, calling to Sir George Lisle, (who was in discourse, and heard not what was declared by Ewers) they and Sir Bernard Gasquoine went away with him, leaving the rest of the gentlemen with sympathizing souls fighting prayers for them, for they might well imagine what evil was intended them, though they knew themselves not to have acted any thing deserving of death at the hands of an enemy; however, submit they must, to the mercy of an enemy; and it is a general rule, that the greatest tokens of a generous and noble soul, is never more beautiful shown, than in behaving with good nature and civility to an enemy when subjected to mercy; and which was ever the practice of the most gallant men in the world.

Julius Caesar having vanquished Pompey, his most implacable enemy in the field of battle, pursued him into Egypt, where on his arrival, Pompey's head was presented to him, having been taken off in a treacherous manner by Theodosius, who thought he should thereby have ingratiated himself into the favor of Caesar; but he was disappointed, for, he no sooner beheld it, but, instead of rejoicing at the death of so potent an enemy, he turned aside his head and wept; and being told, that Achillis, an eunuch, and Photius, were the actors of that murder, caused Photius to be apprehended and put to death immediately; the like sentence would also have been executed on the other, had he not fled and taken shelter in the opposite army.

Many other examples of a like sort have I met with, but never any for men to commit murder under colour of mercy.

But what could we expect in a kingdom so heathenishly reformed; when loyal obedience by pretended law was made rebellion, and horrid tyranny placed

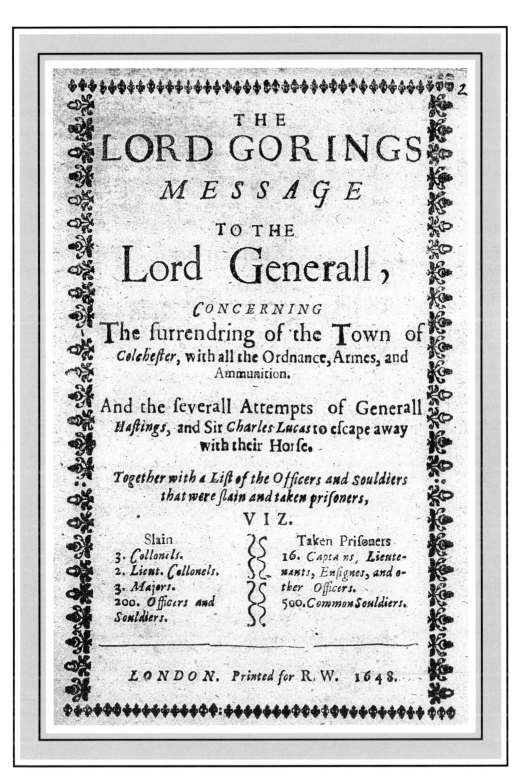

THE
LORD GORINGS
MESSAGE
TO THE
Lord Generall,

CONCERNING

The furrendring of the Town of
Colchefter, with all the Ordnance, Armes, and
Ammunition.

And the feverall Attempts of Generall
Haftings, and Sir *Charles Lucas* to efcape away
with their Horfe.

Together with a Lift of the Officers and Souldiers
that were flain and taken prifoners,

V I Z.

Slain		Taken Prifoners
3. Collonels.		16. Captains, Lieute-
2. Lieut. Collonels.		nants, Enfignes, and o-
3. Majors.		ther Officers.
200. Officers and		500. Common Souldiers.
Souldiers.		

LONDON. Printed for R. W. 1648.

judge of the court; whilst innocent allegiance received its deadly doom at the bar.

The Lords and Gentlemen sat thus expostulating with their discontents, and still revolving in their distracted minds what would be the event; about an hour after which, came a messenger from Sir Charles Lucas, to desire a chaplain might be immediately sent to him; this struck a dead sorrow in the hearts of all. And the Lords (desiring that no man might be a particular sufferer in so general a cause) called up Captain Cannon, an officer of the Parliament's, and entreated him to hasten to the Council of War, and desire them, in the behalf of the prisoners, that they would not make those gentlemen they had taken from them, any greater sufferers than they intended to all; who being all equally concerned in all transactions, it was but just for all to share alike in suffering, more especially as it was their particular desire so to be used.

But all could take no effect in them, having passed their sentence without ever calling the convicted to the court or bar; this was a new unheard of way of condemning men in our nation.

General Fairfax, with his Council of War, were then sitting in the Town Hall,

Fairfax's troops marching past the Old Moot Hall following the surrender of the town.

and the worthy, though unfortunate Knights were locked up in an apartment belonging to the hall, and a strong guard placed at the door. After a short debate in the Council of War, the prisoners were ordered to be brought forth; which being done, they were told by the said Council

"That after so long and obstinate a defence, it was highly necessary, for the example of others, that some military justice should be executed; and therefore, that Council had determined, that they, Sir Charles Lucas, and Sir George Lisle, should be immediately shot to death."

The condemned, though not convicted Knights, were immediately conducted to the Castle, which was then a dungeon, and the County Goal. Soon after which, Colonel Ireton coming to them, said, "they must prepare themselves for death; for, that the sentence which had been passed, was to be executed upon them directly." Sir Charles Lucas asked him, "By what law they were to die; or whether by an ordinance of Parliament, by the Council of War, or by command of the General?" To which Ireton made this answer,

Fairfax entering the Moot Hall

"That it was by vote of the Council of War, according to an order of Parliament; by which order, all that were found in arms, were to be proceeded against as traitors."

Then Sir Charles Lucas replied, "Alas, you deceive yourselves! me you cannot; we are conquered, and must be what you please to make us." Which words he expressed with a countenance as cheerful as one going to a banquet, rather than death, not showing the least symptom of fear; but as it were, scorning death as much as he did the instruments who pronounced his sentence. He then desired time till next morning, in order to settle some things in this world, and to sit and prepare his soul for another; but that request being denied him, he went on again as follows:

"Sir, do not think I make this request out of any desire I have to live, or escape the death you have sentenced me to, for I scorn to ask life at your hand; but that I might have time to make some addresses to God above, and settle some things below, that I might not be hurried out of this world with all my sins about me; but, since your charity will not grant it, I must submit to the mercy of God, whose holy will be done.
Do your worst; I shall soon be ready for execution."

Sir George Lisle said very little, only in like manner, desired a little respite, that he might have time to write to his father and mother, but was also denied that favour. These were true Servants to their old Master, and good practitioners in his doctrine, who thought it not enough to destroy the body, but, as much as in them lay, to kill the soul also.

Colonel Ireton then took leave of the prisoners, and, as an antidote for the poison intended for them, they went to prayers; and both breathed forth such zealous expressions, and heavenly ejaculations, that they seemed already translated into the other world, whilst yet alive. They afterwards prayed with the Chaplain, and received the Blessed Sacrament.

This religious devotion was scarce ended, before they were hurried out of the castle, and conducted to a green spot of ground on the north-side of the said castle, a few paces from the wall, where they were received by three files of musqueteers who were to despatch them.

Sir Charles Lucas and Sir George Lisle descending the Great Staircase of
Colchester Castle prior to their execution.

At the place of execution, those two gallant English Worthies were met by the three following Colonels, viz, Ireton, Rainsborow, and Whaley, who were appointed to be actors, as well as spectators in this inhuman tragedy.

They found the loyal Gentlemen ready to be sacrificed, appearing with as undaunted a resolution to receive their death wound, as they had often before dared it in the field of battle, where the boldest rebel never gained the least trophy of honor, by questioning their gallantry.

Sir Charles Lucas was fixed upon to be the first who was to receive this honor of martyrdom, and on being placed for that purpose, said,

"I have often looked death in the face in the field of battle, and you shall now see I dare die."

He then again fell upon his knees, in which posture he remained a few minutes, and then rose up, and with a cheerful countenance, opened his doublet, and showed them his breast, and then placing his hands by his side, called out to his executioners, "See, I am ready for you, and now, "rebels, do your worst."

At the pronouncing of which words, they fired at him, and, wounding him in several parts of the body, he fell down dead without speaking a word more.

During the execution of Sir Charles Lucas, his friend and fellow sufferer, Sir George Lisle, was conveyed a short distance off, that he might not see him fall; which being over, he was brought to the same place, for the conclusive part of this bloody scene to be performed. Sir George, on viewing the dead body of his friend, (which then lay bleeding on the ground) kneeled down, and kissed him, uttering a funeral elegy in praise of his extraordinary parts, and unspotted honor.

Then standing up, he took out of his pocket, five pieces of gold, which was all the money he had about him, one he gave to be distributed amongst his executioners, and the other four to a person who stood near him, who had some years before been his servant. He desired the said person to deliver the money to his friends in London as his last legacy; concluding with some filial expressions of duty to his father and mother, and recommendations to some particular friends.

He then turned to the spectators, and said as follows,

"Oh! How many of your lives who are now present here, have I saved in hot blood, and must now myself be most barbarously murdered in cold! But what wicked act dare they not do, who would willingly cut the throat of my dear King, whom they have already imprisoned; for whose deliverance and the peace of this miserable and unhappy nation, I shall dedicate these my last prayers to Heaven."

Sir George then looking those who were to execute him in the face, and thinking they stood at too great a distance to do their work completely, desired them to come nearer towards him; to which one of them answered, "I'll warrant ye, Sir, we'll hit you." Upon which, Sir George smiling, said, "I have been nearer you, when you have missed me."

He then kneeled down to prayers some minutes, and after uttering many

The execution of Sir Charles Lucas and Sir George Lisle behind the north wall of Colchester Castle on 28th August, 1648

VNDER THIS
MARBLE LY THE
BODIES OF THE
TWO MOST VALI
ANT CAPTAINS
S^R CHARLES
LVCAS AND S^R
GEORGE LISLE
KNIGHTS WHO
FOR THEIR EMI
NENT LOYALTY
TO THEIR SOVE
RAIN WERE ON
THE 28TH DAY OF AV
GVST 1648 BY THE
COMMAND OF S^R
THOMAS FAIR
FAX THEN GENE
RAL OF THE PAR
LIAMENT ARMY IN
COLD BLOVD BARBA
ROVSLY MVRDERD

The grave slab of Lucas and Lisle in St. Giles' Church

invocations in the name of Jesus Christ, rose up, and said, "I am now ready; traitors, do your worst." Which words were hardly out of his mouth, before they fired at him, and some of the shot going through his body, he dropped dead.

The dead bodies of those gentlemen were conveyed to St. Giles's Church, in Colchester, and both interred in a vault in the north-isle of the said church, belonging to the noble family of the Lucas's; over whose bodies, (after the restoration of King Charles the Second) a large flat marble stone was laid, at the expense of the Lord Lucas, brother to the deceased Sir Charles Lucas; with the following inscription thereon, cut in letters very deep and large, to prevent the wearing them out, if possible, by time, or any other accident.

Sir Bernard Gasquoine, was also ordered to be shot to death at the same time, and in the same place, where Sir Charles Lucas and Sir George Lisle suffered, and received his sentence from the same Council of War.

Sir Bernard Gasquoine was a gentleman of Florence; and had served the King in the war, and afterwards remained in London, till the unhappy adventure of Colchester, and then accompanied his friends thither; and being brought to the place of execution, had only English enough to make himself understood, that he desired a pen, ink, and paper, that he might write a letter to his Prince, the great Duke, and that his highness might know in what manner he lost his life, to the end his heirs might possess his estate. The officer that attended the execution thought fit to acquaint the General and Council, without which he durst not allow him pen and ink, which he thought he might reasonably demand: when they were informed of it, they thought it a matter worthy some considera- tion; they had chosen him out of the list for his quality, conceiving him to be an English gentle- man; and preferred him for being a Knight, that they might sacrifice three of that rank.

After a consultation held, Sir Bernard was

Sir Bernard Gasquoine

ordered to be brought back, and kept with the prisoners, most of the Council of War being of opinion, that if they took away the life of a foreigner, who seemed to be a person of quality, their friends or children, who should visit Italy, might pay dear for many generations.

The two worthy Knights, who were thus murdered, as before related, were men of great name and esteem in the war; the one being held as good a commander of horse, and the other of foot, as the nation had; but of different tempers and humors.

Sir Charles Lucas was the younger brother of the Lord Lucas, and his heir both to the honor and estate, and had a present fortune of his own. He had been bred in the Low Countries under the Prince of Orange, and always amongst the horse. He was very brave in his person, and in a day of battle, a gallant man to look upon, and follow.

Sir George Lisle was a gentleman who had the same education with the other; and at the same time an officer of foot; had all the courage of the other, and led his men to a battle with such an alacrity, that no man was ever better followed, his soldiers never forsaking him; and the party which he commanded, never left any thing undone which he led them upon; but then, to his fierceness of courage, he had the softest and most gentle nature imaginable, was kind to all, and beloved by all, and without a capacity to have an enemy.

The manner of taking away the lives of these two worthy men, was without example, and concluded by all men to be very barbarous, and was generally imputed to Ireton, who swayed the General, and was, upon all occasions, of an unmerciful and bloody nature.

This bloody sacrifice being ended, Fairfax, with the chief officers went to visit the prisoners; and the General (who was an ill orator, on the most plausible occasions) applied with his civility to the Earl of Norwich, and the Lord Capell; seeming in some degree to excuse the having done that, which he said, "the military justice required:" he told them, "That all the lives of the rest were safe, and that they should be well treated, and disposed of as the Parliament should direct."

The Lord Capell had not so soon digested this so late barbarous proceeding, as to receive a visit from those who caused it, with such a return as his condition might have prompted to him; but said, "That the General should have received their thanks, if he had saved the lives of those two worthy Knights who had been executed, and which they valued more than their own; that as they were equally concerned, and acted alike in the engagement and management of the whole affair, they should have shared one fate; and that therefore, Sir Thomas Fairfax, and the Officers would do well to finish their work, by executing the same rigour on the rest."

This answer was very displeasing to Fairfax, and the other officers; Ireton in particular seemed under much discontent thereat; and several sharp and bitter expressions passed between Ireton and his Lordship, and which cost his Lordship his life in a few months after.

The Lords, with some other Gentlemen were then drawn out, and conducted to Mr. Warren's house, over against the King's Head; before which time, the Lords and Gentlemen were all kept in one room, and if any stepped out of the said room into any other, they were stripped naked by the unruly soldiers belonging to the Parliament army.

This being done, Sir Thomas Fairfax gave the Parliament an account of his proceedings, by a letter which he wrote to the Earl of Manchester, the day after the

Sir Henry Ireton.

surrender of the town, an exact copy of which follows, as printed by authority the same year.

To the Right Honorable the Earl of Manchester, Speaker of the Honorable House of Peers.

My Lord,

"I HAVE herewith sent you the Articles, with the explanations annexed, upon which it hath pleased God, in his best time, to deliver the town of Colchester, and the enemy therein, into your hands without further bloodshed, seeing that for some satisfaction to military justice, and in part of avenge for the innocent blood they have caused to be spilt, and the trouble, damage and mischief they have brought upon the town, this country and the kingdom, I have, with the advice of a Council of War, of the chief Officers, both of the country forces and the army, ordered two of them who were rendered at mercy, to be shot to death before any of them had quarter assured them. The persons pitched upon for this example, were Sir Charles Lucas, and Sir George Lisle; in whose military execution, I hope your Lordships will not find cause to think your honor or justice prejudiced. As for the Lord Goring, Lord Capell, and the rest of the persons rendered to mercy, and now assured of quarter, of whose names I have sent your Lordships a particular list, I do hereby render to the Parliament's judgement for further public justice and mercy, to be used as you shall see cause. I desire God may have the glory of his multiplied mercies towards you and the kingdom, at this kind, and in the condition of instruments as to the service here, the Officers and Soldiers of Essex and Suffolk, (who in this time of so dangerous defection, have adhered constantly to yours and the kingdom's interest) for their faithful demeanour and patient indurance in the hardships of this service are not to be forgotten.

"Your Lordships
"Most humble servant,

HYTHE
August 29th, 1648.

T. FAIRFAX."

The Rev. Mr. Spragg, who was Chaplain to Sir Thomas Fairfax, and wrote Anglia Rediviva; or, The Conduct of the Parliament Army under Fairfax, gives the following character of Sir Charles Lucas.

"He was an active Enemy and good Soldier; when Governor of Berkley Castle, and summoned to surrender, he returned this answer, I will eat horseflesh before I will yield; and when that is done, man's flesh. He was a Soldier of reputation and valour."

And he accordingly proved very successful in the defence of that castle, and surrendered to Colonel Rainsborow upon honorable terms, after a storm.

He did great execution with part of his regiment, betwixt Slymbridge and Beverston Castle, upon Colonel Massey's garrison.

He also forced his way through the rebels quarters at Cawood Castle, in the most valiant and courageous manner, insomuch that his name ever afterwards became a terror to his enemies.

His gallant behaviour at Marston Moor will likewise never be forgotten, where he gave the great General Fairfax so fatal a blow, that he could never forgive him; and for which stroke, in revenge, it is thought, he took away his life at Colchester, having often been heard to threaten him.

The brave deportment and admirable behaviour of Sir George Lisle, in like manner, will ever redound to his lasting honor: he behaved with great valour and resolution at Bramdeane Heath.

His incomparable gallantry betwixt Newbury and Spine, will never be forgotten; an account whereof is here inserted, as taken from an impartial and sincere hand.

"As for Colonel Lisle, we want language to express his carriage; for he did all things with as much judgment, cheerfulness, and expedition, as had a particular influence on every common soldier, taking the utmost care of all, excepting himself: In short, he gave the rebels three most gallant charges; in the first, his word to the men under his command in the field of battle, was, For THE CROWN; and they fell on the enemy with the utmost fury, and after firing, beat them down with bullets and musquet shot, and with the butt-ends of their pieces; his field word for the second charge was, FOR PRINCE CHARLES; at which they fell on gallantly, cutting and hewing down numbers of the enemy, and a great many did run away; His third field word was, FOR THE DUKE OF YORK; which proved a finishing stroke, for he charged them so home, that those who were not killed, ran away, and never faced him more; and he declared, that had they stood his attacks, he intended to have charged in the names of all the King's children, till he had not left one rebel alive in the field to fight against the Crown, or the Royal Progeny.

In which engagement the Colonel had no armour on, beside courage and a good cause, and a Holland shirt; for as he seldom wore defensive arms, so he now pulled off his buff-doublet, intending thereby to animate his men, the commonest soldier seeing himself better armed than his Colonel; and as it was dark when they engaged, they might the better discern him from whom they were to receive direction and courage."

But to return: Upon reading Fairfax's letter in the House of Commons, a resolute gentleman stood up, and said, "Mr. Speaker, I know, notwithstanding what is otherwise pretended in this letter, that neither the town of Colchester, nor county of Essex, desired any severity to be used towards those gentlemen, nor are they satisfied therewith; and therefore, I suppose, the pretence of justice, mentioned in Fairfax's letter, was wholly an act of revenge."

To this, no reply was made, but frowns and foul looks, implying their disgust.

Another gentleman also stood up, and was bold enough to say these words: "I am of opinion, that the executing these two Knights now, was done on purpose to put an affront upon the treaty, and to grieve and exasperate his Majesty."

But lest honesty should grow too confident, and thereby be encouraged to speak what they were unwilling to hear, a debate was resumed, which way to dispose of, and proceed against those Lords and others who were rendered to the mercy of the Parliament; after which, proper instructions were dispatched to Fairfax, who had not been idle all this time, for as soon as he had sent the aforesaid letter to the Parliament, he laid a fine of thirteen thousand pounds on the inhabitants of Colchester, with which sum he purposed to pay the army. What sums were paid in Head and North Wards, follows; but those paid in East and South Wards could not be learned, though it is allowed, the money collected, fell short of what was demanded.

The Names of those who paid Fines upon the Surrender of Colchester.

Head Ward.

To   Captain BLACKWELL

		£.	s.	d.
Mr. BUCKSTONE		500.	0.	0.
,,	THURSTON	500.	0.	0.
,,	JEREMY DANIEL	145.	0.	0.
,,	BRACHIM	80.	0.	0.
,,	WILLIAM LORAM	10.	0.	0.
,,	FRANCIS BOROWS	100.	0.	0.
,,	RICHARD STREET	10.	0.	0.
,,	SAMUEL MOOT	200.	0.	0.
,,	ROBERT MOOT	100.	0.	0.
,,	THOMAS MOOT	100.	0.	0.
Mrs.	PELHAM	100.	0.	0.
Mr.	JOHN BREASYER	100.	0.	0.
,,	EDWARD BREASYER	25.	0.	0.
,,	HENRY LAMBE	200.	0.	0.
,,	WILLIAM COACKARELL	30.	0.	0.
,,	WILLIAM BOND, sen.	25.	0.	0.
,,	JAMES BOND	25.	0.	0.
,,	HINMARSH	66.	13.	4.
Mr.	RICHARD STONE	100.	0.	0.
,,	PALMER	20.	0.	0.
,,	HEAVENS	25.	0.	0.

„	JOHN SIMSON	20.	0.	0.
„	JOHN EMENS	10.	0.	0.
„	HENRY LAMB, Draper	25.	0.	0.
Mrs.	PORTLAR	30.	0.	0.
Mr.	CREFIELD SENYAR	200.	0.	0.
Mr.	WILLIAM DOUNES	40.	0.	0.
„	DANET	125.	0.	0.
„	WILLIAM CADMAN	10.	0.	0.
„	RICHARD DANIELL	10.	0.	0.
„	RICHARD BUSHER	35.	0.	0.
„	JOHN BROWN	25.	0.	0.
„	BEALES	100.	0.	0.
„	RICHARD HAWSKBEE	25.	0.	0.
„	ALEXANDER HINMARSH	33.	6.	8.

To Captain EVESTON

Mrs.	LEMING,	100.	0.	0.
Mr.	PETER JOHNSON,	20.	0.	0.
„	ROBINSON,	30.	0.	0.
		Total, 3300	0.	0.

North Ward

To Capt. BLACKWALL.

Mr.	WILLIAM LAMBARD	30.	0.	0.
„	MILLS ADAMS	25.	0.	0.
„	GEORGE HARRISON	50.	0.	0.
„	MATTHEW BROWNE	50.	0.	0.
„	SAMUEL CROUCH	20.	0.	0.
„	WILLIAM SMIGHT	10.	0.	0.
„	GEORGE ROYSARD	10.	0.	0.
„	HUMARSTON	100.	0.	0.

„	John Woodroffe	50.	0.	
„	Humphrey Merrydell	130.	0.	0.
„	Matthew Alyston,	80.	0.	0.

To Captain Cooke.

Mr. John Woodcake,	8.	0.	0.
„ Arthur Candour,	80.	0.	0.

North Ward,	Total, 643.	0. 0.
Head Ward,	Total, 3300.	0. 0.
	Total in full, 3943.	0. 0.

The General then distributed the officers, to every regiment a certain number of gentlemen who were prisoners, as slaves to the gallies, to ransom themselves, and most of them did afterwards purchase their liberties, by giving as much as they were able for the same, and returned home, in which manner they disposed of the greatest part, excepting those who bore a principle command.

The private soldiers and inferior officers, were drawn from the line, and shut up in the churches, where they immediately placed guards over them, and gave free liberty to their foot soldiers to go and pillage them; so that in a very short time there were very few or none left with any cloaths on them, and hardly shirts; and after having thus pillaged and stript them, they marched them away, in a day, when it rained violently, and conducted them from place to place in the country, lodging them in churches, and such places, till many of them were starved, and divers, who could not march by reason of their faintness, they pistolled in the highways, and some they sold (as before they did the Scots) to be transported into foreign countries, from their wives and children, no matter to what part of the world, so they were once gone.

Prodigious numbers were also conveyed to several prisons, as far distant from their homes, as they could contrive; some to Windsor, others to Oxford, Lynn in Norfolk, Warwick, Pendennis, and St. Michael's Mount in Cornwall, Arundel Castle in Sussex, Gloucester, Hereford, Cardiff in Glamorganshire, and other places.

The Lord Capell, and the Earl of Norwich, were soon after removed to Windsor

Castle, where they were kept prisoner till the 7th day of March following, and then brought to trial in the Painted Chamber in Westminster Hall.

The JUDGES were as follows:

JOHN BRADSHAW, Sergeant at Law,
RICHARD KEABLE, dit.
JOSEPH PULLISTON, dit.
MATTHEW SHEPPERD,
WILLIAM UNDERWOOD,
JOHN HAYES,
GEORGE LANGHAM,
GEORGE MANLEY,
JOHN LUNGLEY,
SAMUEL MOYS,
MAURICE THOMPSON,
RICHARD SHUT,
MARK HILDERSEY,
THOMAS ALLEN,
DANIEL TAYLOR,
EDMUND WARREN,
NATH. LACEY,
JOHN STONE,
CORNELIOUS COOK,
WILLIAM WYBEARD,
JOS. BLACKWELL, Esq.
WILLIAM PENROY, ditto.
FRANCIS HACKER ditto,
THO. SAUNDERS, ditto,
THO. TICHBURN, ditto,
THO. BROWNE, ditto,
WILLIAM BARLET, ditto,
WILLIAM HUBBARD, Esq.
SAMP. SHEFFIELD, ditto,
JAMES PRINCE,
NATH. WHETTAM,
SILVANUS TAYLOR,

THOMAS AYRES,
EDWARD CRESSET,
Sir W. BARKHAM, Barrister,
RALPH HARRISON,
MAXMILLAN BEARD,
Sir WILLIAM ROT,
JOHN WHITBY,
JOHN HARRISON,
RICHARD DOUNES,
RICHARD SPARROW,
WILLIAM WEBB,
THOMAS COOK,
ROBERT TICHBOURN,
GEORGE COOPER,
OWEN ROE,
THOMAS PRIDE,
JOHN HUSON,
THOMAS ANDREWS, Alderman,
WILLIAM SPENCE,
JOSIAS BARNARS,
JOSIAS HARDWICK,
ROBERT NORWOOD,
STEPHEN ESTWICK,
THOMAS NOWELL,
THOMAS ARNOLD,
THOMAS AYRE,
Sir J. THOROWGOOD, Kt.
VINCENT POTTER,
WILLIAM PARKER,
SOLOMEN SMITH,
NICHOLAS MARTIN,
Sir R. SALTINGHALL.

124

The Earl of Norwich behaved himself with great submission to the Court, and with all those addresses as were most like to reconcile his Judges to him, and to prevail over their affections; he spoke as follows: "Of his being bred up in the court from his cradle in the time of Queen Elizabeth, of his having been a servant to King James all his reign; of his dependence upon Prince Henry; afterwards upon the late King; of his obligations he had to the Crown, and his endeavours to serve it." And concluded as a man that would be beholden to them if they would give him leave to live.

The Lord Capell appeared undaunted, and utterly refused to submit to their jurisdiction: "That in the condition and capacity of a soldier and a prisoner of war, he said, the lawyers and gown men had nothing to do with him, and therefore he would not answer any thing which they had said against him." (Steele having treated him with great rudeness and insolence) but insisted upon "the law of nations, which exempted all prisoners, though submitting to mercy, from death, if it was not inflicted within so many days; which were long since expired. He urged the declaration which Fairfax the General made to him, and the rest of the prisoners, after the death of Sir Charles Lucas and Sir George Lisle, that no other of their lives should be in danger, which he had witnesses ready to prove, if they might be admitted." And concluded, "That if he had committed any offence worthy of death, he might be tried by his Peers; which was his right by the laws of the land, the benefit whereof he required." Ireton, who was present, and sat as one of the Judges, denied that the General had made any such promise; and if he had, that the Parliament's authority could not be restrained thereby, and put him in mind of his carriage at that time, and how much he neglected the General's civility. The other insisted still on the promise, and urged, that the General might be sent for and examined; which they knew not how to deny; but in regard of the indisposition of his health: they said they would send to him; which they accordingly did.

But whether the question was well stated to Fairfax, or what was else said to him to dissuade him from owning his declaration and promise, he boggled so much in his answer, that they would be of opinion, that he had not made such direct and positive promise; and that the same was never transmitted to the Parliament, which it ought to have been; and that, at most, it could but exempt those prisoners from being tried before a Court, or a Council of War, and could not be understood as an obligation upon the Parliament, not to give direction to such a legal proceeding against him, as they should find necessary for the peace and safety of the kingdom. The President Bradshaw told the Lord Capell, with many insolent expressions; "That he was tried before Judges as the Parliament thought fit to assign him, and who had judged a better man than himself." So sentence of death was pronounced against him; viz. That he should lose his head.

The prisoner was carried to St. James's, where he was to remain until the execution, which was two days after; which time his friends and relations had to endeavour to preserve his life, by the authority of the Parliament; where there were many sitting, who had not sat in judgement upon him: They left no way untried to prevail; offered and gave money to some who were willing to receive it, and made promises accordingly. But they who had the greatest credit, and most power to terrify others, who should displease them, were inexorable: yet dealt so much more honorably than the rest, that they declared to those who solicited for him, that they would not endeavour to do him service. Ireton, above all men, continued his insolent and dogged humor, and told them, "If he had credit, he should die." Others, who gave better words, had no better meaning than he.

The Earl of Norwich came next upon the stage, who always lived a cheerful and jovial life without contracting many enemies, had many there who wished him well, and few who had animosity against

John Bradshaw

him, so that when the question was put concerning him, the house was equally divided, the votes which rejected his Petition, and those who would preserve his life, were equal; so that his life or death depended upon the single vote of the Speaker; who told the House, "That he had received many obligations; and that once when he had been like to have incurred the King's displeasure, by some misinformation, which would have been very penal to him, the Lord Goring, (under which style he was treated, the additional of Norwich not being allowed by them upon their old rule) had by his credit preserved him, and removed the prejudice that was against him; and therefore he was obliged in gratitude to give his vote for the saving him." By this fortune he came to be preserved; whether the ground of it were true or no, or whether the Speaker made it only as an excuse to save a man's life who was put to ask it in that place.

Lord Capel escaping from the Tower of London.

The Lord Capell, shortly after he was brought prisoner to the Tower, from Windsor Castle, had by a wonderful adventure, having a cord and all things necessary conveyed to him, let himself down out of the window of his chamber in the night, over the wall of the Tower; and had been directed through what part of the ditch he might be best able to wade; but whether he found the right place, or whether there was no safer place, he found the water and the mud so deep, that had he not been by the head taller than other men, he must have perished, since the water came up to his chin.   The way was so long on the other side, and the fatigue of drawing himself out of so much mud was so intolerable, that his spirits was near spent, and he was ready to call out for help, as thinking it better to be carried back to prison, than to be found in such a place, from whence he could not extricate himself, and where he was ready to expire.   But it pleased God that he got at last to the other side, where his friends expected him, and carried him to a chamber in the Temple, where he remained two or three nights secure from any discovery, notwithstanding the diligence that could not but be used to recover a man they designed to use no better.

After two or three days, a friend whom he trusted much, and who deserved to be trusted; conceiving that he might be more secure in a place to which there was less resort, and where there were so many harboured who were every day sought after, had provided a lodging for him at a private house at Lambeth Marsh; and calling upon him in the evening, when it was dark, to go thither, they chose rather to take any boat they found at the Temple Stairs, than to trust one of those people with the secret; and then it was so late, that there was only one boat left there.   In that the Lord Capell, (as well disguised as he thought necessary) and his friends put themselves, and bid the waterman to row them to Lambeth: whether in their passage thither, the other gentlemen called him, my Lord, as was confidently reported; or, whether the waterman had any jealousy by observing what he thought a disguise, when they were landed, the wicked waterman, undiscerned, followed them, till he saw in what house they went; and then went to an officer, and demanded, what would he give him to bring him to the place where the Lord Capell lay? and the officer promising to give him ten pounds, he led him presently to the house, where that excellent person was seized upon, and the next day carried to the Tower.

When the Petition, that his wife had delivered, was read, many gentlemen spoke in his behalf; and mentioned the great virtues that were in him; and that he had never deceived them, or pretended to be of their party; but always resolutely declared himself for the King.   And Cromwell, who had known him very well, spoke so much good of him that all men thought he was now safe, when he concluded,   "That his affection to the Public so much weighed down his private friendship, that he could not but tell them, that the question was now, whether they would preserve the most bitter and most implacable enemy they had?   That he knew the Lord Capell very well, and knew that he would be the last man in England who would forsake the Royal interest; that he had great courage, industry and generosity, that he had many friends who would always adhere to him; and that as long as he lived, what condition soever he was in, he would be a thorn in their sides; and therefore, for the good of the Common Wealth, he would give his vote against the Petition. Ireton's hatred was immortal, he spoke of him, and against him, as of a man whom he heartily was afraid of.

My Lord Capell finding that his friends had made what intercession they could to get his pardon, but all to no purpose, and the time of his suffering being near at hand, and no expectation of his life, he wrote two letters to his disconsolate Lady, the contents whereof are as follows:

Oliver Cromwell

THE LETTER HE SENT TO HIS LADY THE DAY BEFORE HIS EXECUTION.

My dearest Life,

"MY greatest care in relation to the world, is for thy dear self, But, I beseech thee, that as thou hast never refused my advice hitherto, do thou now consummate all in this one: and indeed it is so important both to thee, me, and all our children, that I presume passion shall not over-rule thy reason, and my request. I beseech thee, again and again, moderate thy apprehension and sorrows for me, and thereby preserve thyself to the benefit of our dear Children, whom God of his love in Christ Jesus hath given us; and our dear Molly (in the case she is in) and our comforts in that family, depend entirely upon thy preservation. I pray remember, that the occasion of my death, will give thee more cause to celebrate my memory with praise, rather than to consider it with sadness. God had commanded my obedience to the Fifth Commandment, and for acting that duty I am condemned. I shall leave thee my Children; in them to live with thee; and leave thee to the protection of a most gracious God.

And I rest, "Thy dear Husband, &c."

THE FOLLOWING LETTER HE SENT TO HIS LADY ON THE DAY OF HIS EXECUTION.

My dearest Life,

"MY eternal life is in Christ Jesus, my worldly consideration in the highest degree thou hast deserved. Let me live long here in thy dear memory, to the comfort of my Family, our dear Children, whom God out of mercy in Christ hath bestowed on us. I beseech thee take care of thy health; sorrow not unsoberly, unusually. God be unto thee better than an husband, and to my Children better than a father. I am sure he is able to be so; I am confident, he is graciously pleased to be so. God be with thee, my most virtuous Wife: God multiply many comforts to thee and my Children, is the fervent prayer of

"Thy dear Husband, &c."

On the Lord Capell's being called, he walked through Westminster Hall, saluting such of his friends and acquaintance as he saw there, with a serene countenance, accompanied by his friend Dr. Morley, who had been with him from the time of his sentence; but at the foot of the scaffold, the soldiers stopping the Doctor, his Lordship took his leave of him, and embracing him; said, "He should go no further;" having some apprehension that he might receive some affront by that rude people after his death, the Doctor being well known to be a friend to the Royal Family, and an opposer of the proceedings of the Parliament.

As soon as his Lordship had ascended the scaffold, he looked very vigorously about; and asked, "Whether the other Lords had spoken to the people with their hats on?" and being told that they were all bare; he then with a clear and strong voice, said, "That he was brought thither to die for doing that which he could not repent of: That he had been born and bred under the government of a King whom he was bound in conscience to obey; under laws to which he had been always obedient; and in the bosom of a church which he thought the best in the world: That he never violated his faith to either of those, and was now condemned to die against all the laws of the land; to which sentence he did submit."

He enlarged himself in commending the great virtue and piety of the King, whom they had put to death, who was so just and merciful a Prince, and prayed to God to forgive the nation that innocent blood. Then he recommended to them Prince Charles; who, he told them, "was their true and lawful Sovereign, and was worthy to be so: That he had the honor to be some years near his person, and therefore assured them he could not but know him well;" and told them, "that he was a Prince of great understanding, of an excellent nature, of great courage, an entire lover of justice, and of exemplary piety: That he was not to be shaken in his religion, and had all those princely virtues which could make a nation happy; and therefore advised them to submit to his government, as the only means to preserve themselves, their posterity, and the protestant religion."

Now having shown the honor and integrity he had for his Royal Master and his Son, who though in exile, was then our present King; he desired that he might have time to prepare himself for the other world; and said, "He suffered as many others had done before him, in the defence of our Royal Martyr, whose virtues were inexpressible." Then turning about, and looking for the Executioner, who was gone off the scaffold, said, "Which is the gentleman? Which is the man?" Answer was made, "He is coming." He then said, "Stay! I must put off my doublet first, and my waistcoat." Then the Executioner being come upon the scaffold, the Lord Capell said, O friend! Prithee come hither:" Then the Executioner kneeling down, the Lord Capell said, "I forgive thee from my soul; and not only forgive thee, but I shall pray to God to give thee all grace for a better life. There is five pounds for thee; as for my cloaths and other effects, if there be anything due to you on that account, you shall be fully recompensed; but I desire my body may not be stripped here, but delivered to my servants; and I also desire, that when I lie down, you would allow me time for a particular short prayer; and when I lift up my right hand, you may strike the blow.

His Lordship then went to the front of the scaffold, and said as follows:

FRIENDS AND COUNTRYMEN,

"THE Conclusion I made with those who sent me hither, and are the cause of this violent death of mine, shall be the beginning of what I shall say to you. In my last address to them, with much sincerity I told them, that I would pray to the God of all mercies, that they might be partakers of his inestimable and boundless mercies in Jesus Christ; and I yet continue that prayer; and beseech the God of Heaven to forgive the injury they have done me. This I do from my soul; and think it my duty to do as a Christian. It is also necessary to tell you further, that I am a Protestant; which I sincerely declare I am, and much in love with the profession of it, after the manner of being established in England, by the Thirty-nine Articles: It is a blessed religion, and I solemnly declare, I never knew any so good. I mention this to clear myself from a malicious aspersion flung upon me, viz. That I am a Papist. I love and commend good works, but believe they are not sufficient matters for Salvation. My anchor-hold is, That Christ loved me, and gave himself for me. And this I rest upon.

I shall now fay something to you as a citizen of the world, in which capacity I appear, though am condemned to die, contrary to the law which governs the world; I mean the law of the sword: I had the protection and honor of the sword, engaged for my life, but they have fallen from those promises and engagements: However, I shall say no more on that head. You who are Englishmen, and here present, behold me, your Countrymen, and acknowledged a Peer of the Realm, not condemned to die by any of the laws of England, but (which is more strange) contrary to the laws of this Kingdom. I am to die for maintaining the Fifth Commandment, enjoined by God himself, which commands reverence and obedience to parents: All Divines, though they disagree in other Articles, acknowledge that magistracy and order is here intended; and I have certainly obeyed that magistracy and order, under which I lived, and thought myself bound to pay due obedience unto.

Gentlemen, I think this a fit opportunity to remind you of his Majesty, our last King; who, in my opinion, (and I have made a survey of the conduct and actions of the greatest and virtuous Princes in the World) was the worthiest Gentleman, the best Master, the best Friend, the best Husband, the best Father, and the best Christian, that this age hath produced, being without any kind of vice.

Pray God preserve his Son, and grant him to be more fortunate, and a greater length of days. I was counsellor to him, and lived with him, and never saw greater hopes of virtue in any young person, than in him; of a nature truly honorable; quick apprehension, great judgement, and a perfect Englishman in his inclinations: I pray God restore him to the Crown, unite these Kingdoms, and send prosperity and happiness both to him and you; that he may live long to reign among you; and that, that family may reign till THY KINGDOM COME; that is, while all temporal power is consummated. Once more, I beseech God of his mercy, to grant happiness to this your King, and the greatest and choicest blessings on you his subjects, by the grace of Jesus Christ.

I shall conclude in the manner I began, with hearty Prayers to Almighty God, that he would be graciously pleased to pardon those who are the occasion of my being brought to this untimely death: For, my part, I will not accuse any of them with malice, not knowing of a certainty, whether there was any malice subsisting among them: Nay I will not so much as think they had a malicious view in their proceedings: What ends they aim at, I know not, nor shall I now examine.

To conclude: The Lord of Heaven bless and protect you all: God Almighty be infinite in goodness and mercy to you, and direct you in those ways of obedience to his commands, and those of his Majesty, that this Kingdom may yet be a happy and glorious Nation; and your King will then be happy in so good and obedient a people.

God Almighty keep you all; God Almighty preserve this Kingdom; God Almighty protect you all."

He then kneeled down, and said a short prayer; and rising, went again to the front of the scaffold, and said to the spectators: "Gentlemen, though I make no question of your doing voluntarily what I am going to ask, yet I hope my reminding you of it, will not be taken amiss; it is, that you would all join with me in prayers, in these my last moments, begging that God would mercifully receive my Soul.

Which being promised, he cried out, "O Lord God, I do with a perfect and willing heart, submit to thy will.   O God, I do most willingly humble myself. Pray God bless you all."

And then laying his head over the block, asked the Executioner whether he laid right, who answering Yes, then, said he, "Honest man, strike boldly, for I forgive you from my soul," at which words he held out his right hand, and the Executioner, at one blow, fevered his head from his body.

His head and body were afterwards taken up by his servants, who attended for that purpose, and being put into a coffin, were conveyed to his Lordships house, and after interred in a private manner.

On the day his Lordship was beheaded, he received the blessed sacrament from the hands of Dr. Morley, who had attended him all the time of his confinement. He had continued in prayers all the night before, with strong, hearty and passionate affections; first confessing and bewailing his sins, with cries and tears; secondly, most humbly and earnestly desiring God's mercy, thro' the merits of Christ only; thirdly, for his dear wife and children, with some passion, but for her especially, with most ardent affection; recommending them to the Divine Providence with great confidence and assurance; and desired for them rather the blessings of a better life than of this; behaving all the time with great humility and zeal.

After receiving the sacrament, he appeared very cheerful, and said, "I doubt not but I shall have sufficient strength to walk through the vale of death, in a manner becoming a Christian."

But he was to have an agony before his passion, and that was when he took a final leave of his wife, eldest son, son-in-law, and two of his uncles; especially the parting with his dear lady, which was the saddest spectacle ever beheld; and, on that occasion, he could not forbear showing a tincture of human frailty; yet, even then, he did not forget to comfort and council her, as well as the rest of his friends: Particularly, in bestowing his blessing on the young Lord, he commanded him never to revenge his death, should it be in his power so to do: The like he said unto his Lady: He told his son, he would leave him a legacy out of David's Psalms; which was this, "Lord, lead me in a plain path;" for, Boy, says he, "I would have you a plain honest man, and a hater of dissimulation."

When his wife, and his other friends and relations were conveyed from him, he said to the Doctor Morley: "Now, Doctor, the hardest piece of work I had to perform in this world, is past;" meaning, the taking a final leave of his wife.

Thus was the British nation deprived of the most noblest champion it had; he was a man in whom the malice of his enemies could discover very few faults, and whom his friends could not with better accomplished; whom Oliver Cromwell's own character well described, add who indeed would never have been contented to have lived under that government.

His memory all men loved and reverenced, though few followed his example.

He had always lived in a state of great plenty, and general estimation, having a very noble fortune of his own by descent, and a fair addition to it by his marriage with an excellent wife, a lady of very worthy extraction, of great virtue and beauty, by whom he had a numerous issue of both sexes, in which he took great joy and comfort, so that no man was more happy in all his domestic affairs; and he was so much the more happy, in that he thought himself most blessed in them.

And yet the King's honor was no sooner violated, and his just power invaded, than he threw all those blessings behind him; and having no other obligations to the Crown, than those which his own honor and conscience suggested to him, he frankly engaged his person and his fortune, from the beginning of the troubles, as many others did, in all actions and enterprises of the greatest hazard and danger; and continued to the end, without ever making one false step, as few others did, though he had once, by the iniquity of a faction, that then prevailed, an indignity put upon him which might have excused him for some remission of his former warmth; but it made no other impression upon him, than to be quiet and contented, whilst they would let him alone, and with the same cheerfulness, to obey the first summons, when he was called out; which was quickly after.

In a word, he was a man that whoever shall, after him, deserve best of the English nation, he can never think himself undervalued, when he shall hear, that his courage, virtue, and fidelity, is laid in the balance with, and compared to that of the Lord Capell.

So ended the year One Thousand Six Hundred Forty Eight; a year of reproach and infamy above all years which had passed before it; a year of the highest dissimulation and hypocrisy, of the deepest villainy, and most bloody treasons, that any nation was ever cursed with, or under; a year, in which the memory of all the transactions ought to be rased out of all records, lest, by the success of it Atheism, Infidelity, and Rebellion, should be propagated in the world.

FINIS.

The Obelisk in the Castle Bailey marking the site of the execution of Sir Charles Lucas and Sir George Lisle in 1648.

Subscribers to the 1788 Edition

A.

MR. Abbot, *Colchefter*

Kitty Abrahams, ditto

Capt. Acton, *Maldon*

Mr. Adams, ditto-2 copies.

Mr. Ambrose, *Miftley*

Mrs. Andrews, *Colchefter*

Mr. Askett, *Tollefhunt D'Arcy*

B.

Mr. Balls, *Colchefter*

Mr. Baker, ditto

Mr. W. Barnes, ditto

Mr. J. Barnes, ditto

Mr. Barrett, ditto

Mrs. Beale, ditto

Mr. Bedford, ditto

Mr. Beswick, ditto

Mr. Biscoe, ditto

Mr. Blyth, *Boxted Heath*

Mr. Boggis, *Colchefter*

Mr. Braisted, ditto

Mr. Bridges, ditto

Mr. Brooker, ditto

Mr. Brookes, ditto

Mr. J. Brown, ditto

Mr. Brown, *Colchefter*

Mr. Brown, ditto

Mr. Brown, ditto

Mr. A. Brown, *Chelmsford*

Mr. Bruce, *Colchefter*

Mr. P. Buckingham, ditto

Mr. J. Buckingham, ditto

Mr. Buckingham, ditto

Mr. Budd, ditto

Mr. Bugg, ditto

Mr. Burridge, ditto

Mr. Byford, ditto

C.

Mr. Capps, *Colchefter*

Mr. Carey, ditto

Mr. Catchpool, ditto

Mr. Clachar, *Chelmsford*

Mr. J. Clark, *Colchefter*

Mr. W. Clark, ditto

Mr. Clay, ditto

Mr. Cobbs, *Copford*

Mr. Cockfage, *Maldon*

Mr. Coe, *Colchefter*

Mr. Cook, *Rowhedge*

Mr. Cooper, *Colchefter*

Capt. Craven, ditto

Mr. Creek, ditto

Mr. Crufwell, ditto

Mr. Cutler, ditto

D.

Mr. Dale, *Goldhanger*

Mr. Daniel, *Colchefter*

Mr. Deeks, ditto

Mr. Delight, ditto

Mr. Dennis, ditto

Mr. Denny, ditto

Mrs. Dowfon, ditto

Mr. Dyer, ditto

E.

Mr. Edwards, *Colchefter*

Mr. Emery, ditto
Mr. Everett, ditto

F.

Mr. Fairs, *Colchefter*
Mr. Furgufon, ditto
Mr. Finch, *Colchefter*
Mr. Finney, ditto
Mr. Forguard, *Meffing*
Mr. Franklin, *Colchefter*
Mr. French, ditto
Mr. Frood, *Maldon*

G.

Mr. Garland, *Colchefter*
Mr. Garritt, ditto
Mr. Garwood, *St. Ofyth*
Mr. Gilfon, *Colchester*
Mr. Glyde, ditto
Mr. Goulding, *St. Ofyth*
Capt. Gray, *Sunderland*

H.

Mr. Hale, *Colchefter*
Mr. Hales, *Tollefhunt D' Arcy*
Mr. Hamilton, *Dedham*
Mr. Hammond, *Colchefter*
Mr. Harding, ditto
Mr. Harris, ditto
Mr. Hathaway, ditto
Mr. Hawes, *Merfea*
Mr. A. Hawkins, *Colchefter*
Mr. J. Hawkins, ditto
Mr. Hedge, ditto
Mr. Hewitt, *Merfea*
Mr. Hodges, *Colchefter*
Mr. Hornet, ditto

Mr. Hunt, ditto
Mr. Hutton, ditto

J.

Mr. Jackfon, *Colchefter*
Capt. Jacobs, ditto
Mr. T. Jeffries, ditto
Mr. T. B. Jeffries, ditto
Mr. Johnson, ditto
Mr. W. Johnfon, ditto
Mr. Jones, *London*

K.

Mr. Kendall, *Colchefter*
Mr. King, ditto

L.

Mr. Lake, *St. Ofyth*
Mr. Lane, *Colchefter*
Mr. Large, *Great Clacton*
Mr. T. Lay, *Wivenhoe*
Mr. Levett, *Maldon*
Mr. Lewis, *Colchefter*
Mr. Lews, *Tollefbury*

M.

Mr. Marfden, *Colchefter*
Mr. Mafon, jun. Ditto
Mr. Matthews, ditto
Mr. Miller, *Varley*
Mr. Miller, *Colchefter*
Mr. Mintor, ditto
Mr. Mitchell, *Peldon*
Mr. E. Moore, *Colchefter*
Mr. S. Moore, ditto
Mr. Moore, *Mile-end*

N.

Mr. Norman, *Colchefter*
Mr. Norris, *London*

O.

Mr. Orrin, *Colchefter*
Mr. Osborn, *Wiston, Suffolk*

P.

Mr. Payne, *Colchefter*
Mr. Pearpoint, *Maldon*
Mr. Perry, *Tollesbury*
Mrs. Pickard, *Colchefter*
Mr. Pickefs, *Dedham*
Mr. Picket, ditto
Mr. Pitt, *Colchefter*
Mr. Polley, *Copford*
Mr. Poore, *Nayland*
Mr. Punchard, *Ipfwich*
Mr. Purkefs, *Colchefter*
Mr. Purkins, ditto

R.

Mr. Rackham, *Bury*
Mr. Rawling, *Goldhanger*
Mr. Ray, *St. Ofyth*
Mr. Ray, *Varley*
Mr. Rolph, *Kent's Hill*
Mr. Roufe, *Colchefter*
Mr. Royce, *Tollefbury*
Mrs. Royce, ditto
Mrs. Rudkin, *Colchefter*
Mr. Rudkin, *Coggefhall*

S.

Mr. Sadler, *Colchefter*

Mr. Sadler, *Horkefley*
Mr. Scopes *Meffing*
Mrs. Scot, *Colchefter*
Mr. Searls, ditto
Mr. Serjeant, *Wivenhoe*
Mr. J. Shelton, *Colchefter*
Mr. Shepherd, ditto
Mr. Shearman, ditto
Mr. Shearman, *Dedham*
Mr. Shillito, jun, *Colchefter*
Mrs. Shorey, ditto
Mr. Simmons, ditto
Mr. Smith, ditto
Mr. H. Smith, ditto
Mr. J. Smith, ditto
Mr. Smith, *Tollefhunt D' Arcy*
Mr. Smitheman, *Braintree*
Mr. Snell, *Colchefter*
Mrs. Spurling, ditto
Mr. Staines, *Colchefter*
Mr. Stiles, *Colchefter*
Mr. Stoke, *Witham*
Mr. Stradling, *Colchefter*
Mr. Stubbing, ditto
Mr. Summerfum, ditto

T.

Ensign Thorley, 44th *Regiment of Foot*
Mrs. Tidman, *Thorpe*
Capt. Timmes, 9th. *Regiment of Foot*
Mr. Triggs, *Suffolk*

V.

Mr. Verlander, *Colchefter*

W

Mr. Walton, *Colchefter*
Mr. Ward, *Meffing*
Mr. Warden, *Tollefhunt D' Arcy*
Mr. Warren, *Tollefbury*
Mr. Watson, *Colchefter*
Mr. Waynman, ditto
Mr. Webb, *Wivenhoe*
Mr. Wells, *Maldon*
Mr. Wenlock, *Colchefter*
Mr. Whiley, ditto
Mr. Wiles, ditto
Mr. Wilkin, *Tollefhunt Knights*
Mrs. Wilkinson, *Colchefter*
Mr. Williams, *Boxted*
Mr. Windon, *Goldhanger*
Mr. Winney, *Nayland*
Mr. Winnock, *London*
Mr. Witnall, *Colchefter*
Mr. Witty, ditto
Mr. Woolfey, *Wivenhoe*
Mr. Worts, *Colchefter*
Mr. Wybred, ditto

Y.

Mr. Young, *Colchefter*
Mifs Younghusband, ditto

SUBSCRIBERS TO THIS EDITION

JMH Publications would like to extend their appreciation and gratitude to the many people who subscribed to this work in advance of its publication.

1. The Mayor of Colchester
2. Deirdre & Brian Norman
3. John & Caryl Gardner
4. Nancy Mitchell
5. Graham Hedges
6. Sandra Campbell
7. Alec J. Corton
8. Brian & Gillian Light
9. Mabel & Charles Sallows
10. Miss Ivy Randolph
11. Mrs G. Mary Coe
12. Mrs Jean Blowers
13. Robert Blowers
14. Jim & Dorothy Waller
15. Peter M. Ratcliffe
16. David Craze
17. B.A.B. Barton
18. Robert & Hilda Gilmour
19. Jess Jephcott
20. Rosalind M. Kaye
21. R.F. Burns
22. Hector & Mary Munson
23. Mr T.N. De-Vries
24. Vicky Jane Daniell
25. Bob Russell, MP for Colchester
26. Joseph Russell
27. Heather Read
28. Mike & Barbara Cant
29. Jean & Robert Sheppard
30. Paul R. Sheppard
31. Colchester Archaeological Group
32. Ron & Lorna Greenwold
33. Martin Theobald
34. Mr C. East
35. Stephen & Patricia Hall
36. Frank & Kathleen Thompson
37. John S. Appleby, F.R. Hist. S.
38. Hazel Inkersole
39. The Sixth Form College, Colchester.
40. Derek A.J. & Kathleen Tulley
41. L.C. Leach
42. Mr. & Mrs. K&J. Chilvers
43. Pam & Ian Johnston
44. Barbara Butler
45. Angela Udall
46. Yvonne Turner
47. Sir William Boulton BT
48. Eric & Beryl Jordan
49. Mr. K. Harwood
50. Lorna K. Gray
51. Mary Dale
52. Alison Capp
53. Ann Turner
54. M.A.W. Head, M.B.E., M.A. (Oxen)
55. Betty & Jack Warner
56. University of Essex
57. Nadine Chinnery
58. Anthony Doe
59. Mrs M.J. Claydon
60. M.F. Smith-Howell
61. Mr Philip Holmes
62. Mr A. Whelan, St. Benedicts College
63. St. Benedicts College
64. Joan Clarke
65. Shirley Everitt
66. Mary Razzell
67. Elizabeth & Jessica Watling
68. Ian Baalham
69. Anne & Ray Milburn
70. Jennifer Hughes
71. David J. Appleby, M.A.
72. Alan Lockwood
73. Mrs Eileen Burridge
74. Beryl Cowen
75. Gordon Bailey
76. Jim Lovell

77.	Tom Glover	122.	Christine & John Stimpson
78.	Peter Evans	123.	E. M. Simpson
79.	Paul Jasper	124.	Pam Wilson
80.	Hywel & Pam Edwards	125.	Steve Wright
81.	R. W. Ashby	126.	Joan Cockerill
82.	Miss Alice May Ashby	127.	Harvey & Jill Russell
83.	David & Margaret Appleton	128.	Philip George
84.	Anthony Askew	129.	Mrs Avril Farahar
85.	Daniel Clark	130.	J. A. Bullard
86.	Ruth Clark & Adam Stuart-Box	131.	Beryl Page
87.	Mr & Mrs P.J. Egan	132.	Paul Thompson
88.	Peter Luxmoore	133.	Mrs R.E.G. Perrins
89.	Miss D.C. Fordham, CBE.	134.	Lilian Mary Morrow
90.	Bob & Margaret Fisher	135.	Lawrence Chopping
91.	Bert & Freda Darch	136.	Brian Turner
92.	Peter & Maureen Taylor	137.	James & Shirley Knott
93.	Roy & Paula Munson	138.	Mr Martin L. Gibbs
94.	R. S. Mahendra	139.	Cecil & Felicity Minter
95.	Arthur & Barbara Sycamore	140.	Tony J. Bettis
96.	Edna A. Guest	141.	David M. Green
97.	Mary F. Jones	142.	Nicholas Clarke
98.	Ted Mayes	143.	Mrs Daphne Reed
99.	Jennifer Reynolds	144.	Mr & Mrs Bray
100.	Heather L. Taylor	145.	Mr B.E. Wright & Mrs U.A. Broughton
101.	Eunice S. Payne		
102.	Barbara Tricker	146.	Adam Harrington
103.	Donald Walker	147.	David Lamb
104.	John & Caryl Gardner	148.	Mr P.J. Campbell
105.	Mr & Mrs L. Egner	149.	T. Taylor
106.	Patrick & Barbara Brennan	150.	Nigel Chapman
107.	Evelyn & Eric Potter	151.	Mark Pentney
108.	Bruce Neville	152.	J. & P.C. Phillips
109.	Margaret & Robert Sainty	153.	Richard & Wendy Allen
110.	Barbara Byrne	154.	Jenny & Rodney Ellis
111.	G. E. Bainbridge	155.	Owen B. Hay
112.	Jennifer Pettitt	156.	Jonathan O. Hay
113.	Annie & Tony Liu	157.	Rebecca Hay
114.	Roderick Starkey-Green	158.	Mr & Mrs A.V. Rowley
115.	Bernard & Brenda Neville	159.	Alan Bollington
116.	Derek Folkard	160.	Mrs Barbara Barton
117.	Eileen & George Williams	161.	Mrs Barbara Barton
118.	Victor J. Lewis	162.	Andrew Millar
119.	Stephen W. Corton	163.	Mr & Mrs P.R. Bingham
120.	Eric J. Andrews	164.	Doreen & George Brimm
121.	Mrs Flora B. Alexander	165.	Peter Cole

166. Mr Alan Scopes
167. Eric D. Appleton
168. John R. Chalmers
169. Penny & Peter Stynes
170. Mrs M. Attewell
171. Patrick & Christine Denney
172. Lynette Singers
173. Dr J.A. Benbow
174. Joe McGoldrick
175. Mr & Mrs S.H. Sheppard
176. Derak Smith
177. Jane & Glyn Stanway
178. Mrs Sheila M. Howard
179. D. L. Greenacre
180. Mrs Daphne M. Blacknell
181. P. D. Carter
182. Rosemary Martin
183. Geraldine & Peter Joslin
184. Mrs Doreen Goddard
185. E. Nora & Patrick Girling
186. Dorothy Robinson
187. Derrick & Margaret Barnden
188. Dominic Waggett
189. David James
190. John & Daphne Rose
191. Colchester Central Library
192. Colchester Central Library
193. Colchester Central Library
194. Timothy Jackson
195. Mary & Ivan Hazell
196. Elizabeth A. Williams
197. Marcel Glover
198. Maria & Joseph Milburn
199. B. A. Foster-Smith
200. Kathy Stoev
201. Dr H.J. Wood
202. Carl Greenaway
203. Richard & Patience Ling
204. Mr & Mrs K. Steers
205. Peter & May Hands
206. Kenneth E. & Sheila L. Wakeling
207. Mr & Mrs Leonard Drinkell
208. Sheila & Arthur Livings
209. June & Philip Warburton
210. Kate Sheffield

211. Lyn Barton
212. Sheila & John Herbert
213. E. Marion Pleasance
214. Vivienne & Robert Wheatley
215. Nigel & Janet Austin
216. Hugh Weatherly
217. Christopher Arthur Dyne
218. Nathan Dyne Lawrence
219. Michael Hedges
220. Mr P.T. Lovelock
221. Christina Ford
222. Mr S.B. Doe
223. Mr H.J. Leach
224. Peter & Paul Burridge
225. Chris McConnell
226. Sir Michael Holt
227. M.I. & M.A. Brown
228. Rodney Anderson
229. Mrs M.O. Furnival
230. Mr & Mrs Neil Pugh
231. Miss Anne E. Barker
232. Joyce H. Wrobel
233. Mr William Albert Cooper
234. Mrs M. Clift
235. Harry & Dorothy Winter
236. Beryl & Bruce Ridgers
237. Beryl & Bruce Ridgers
238. Mrs Patricia Wright
239. Colonel Sir Neil Thorne, OBE, TD,DL.
240. Sir George Lisle's Regiment, of
      'The Sealed Knot Society'
241. Mr P.B. Humphrey
242. Mr D.C. Warden
243. Mr & Mrs G. Leimbach
244. Ron Sharp, J.P.
245. Stuart Chamberlain
246. Mrs Angela Mogg
247. Gavan Edward Scully
248. Martin Room
249. Douglas Clayden
250. Lesley Elliott
251. Mrs Marjorie Goodman
252. Gladys Jackson
253. Colchester Masonic Hall Co Ltd

254. Thomas K. Smith, on behalf of the (Lucas & Lisle's Lodge, No.8456)
255. Maureen Somers
256. Mathew Turner
257. Pam Redding
258. Bernard Polley
259. Margaret Pilkington
260. Jane Rees
261. Mrs Doris Graves
262. Bev Adams
263. Sue & Rick
264. Vi Poulson
265. David & June Kirby
266. Mr R. Allington
267. Andrew Phillips
268. Margaret Ann Hedges
269. Stephen, Karen & Gemma Brown
270. Paul Horne
271. Kit & Mary Hughes
272. Mrs Margaret Berry
273. Christine Bowen
274. Mrs Joan L. Coates
275. Mr Michael Coates
276. Julia & Adrian Manley
277. Vivien & Michael Jones
278. Pauline K. Marstrand
279. C. Haines
280. Pamela Harris
281. Dinah James
282. Ian Brice
283. Ian Valentine
284. Charles & Barbara Bolton
285. Mrs Violet Crook
286. Norman Peckston
287. Elizabeth Bright
288. Jack Leather
289. David Baker
290. Kathleen Birkin
291. Reg Silk & Dave Cable

292. Geoff and Ruth Greenwold
293. Mr H. Millatt
294. Peter Tweed
295. Peter Luxmoore
296. Jane and John Rayner
297. Mrs M. Fitch
298. Austin Baines
299. Pauline & Keith Lovell
300. Chris & Sheila Anderton
301. St. James' C of E Voluntary Aided Primary School
302. Mrs June Jones
303. Mrs June Jones
304. Mrs June Jones
305. David and Elly Clark
306. Ken and Mary Pilgrim
307. Dr. F.F. Casale
308. Andrew Wassel
309. Martin J. Corton
310. Andrew Johnston
311. Paul, Isobel Johnston & Family
312. Stephen Crane
313. Mrs Phyllis Richardson
314. Barnard Slack
315. Edward Winney
316. Betty K. Pidgeon
317. Bob Gooden
318. Betty R. Constable
319. Betty Darlow
320. Raymond J. Lee
321. Ann Barry
322. S.A.M. Connal
323. Roger & Linder Frost
324. Mrs E. S. Beere
325. Mrs. J. Gallifent
326. Janet Williams
327. A. E. Anning
328. David T. Wilson

MAP & DIARY
OF
SIEGE OF COLCHESTER

A DIARY of the Siege of COLCHESTER by the Forces under the Command of General FAIRFAX.

Tuesday June 13 1648

The Lord Fairfax engaged in the fields before Colchester, near St. Maries, the Lord Gorings Forces, together with the Forces under Command of the Lord Capell, and Sir Charles Lucas, and beat them into the Town; Sir William Leyton, and between 4 and 500 of ye Kings Forces were taken prisoners, (200 of them being of Colonell Farrs Regiment,) and in pursuit of the reft, Col. Barkeftead, with his Regiment, entred the Suburbs as far as head-Gate, and entred ye Gate, but being overpowered there, and out of the Church-yard, ye Kings Forces Barracadoed the Gate, (leaving neer 500 men to our mercy;) yet not withftanding thofe foot, and Col. Needhams fought many hours after in hopes to gain the Town at that place, but could not, the Kings Forces making good refistance; there were flain of the Kings Forces, Col. Sir William Campion, Col. Cooke, and divers Officers of quality, and about 80 private soldiers; Col. Panton, Capt Brunkerd, Clifford Worsop, and divers other Officers wounded. On General Fairfax's side, Col. Needham, Capt. Lawrence of Horse, Capt. Cox of Foot, and neer 100 private souldiers and inferior Officers were slain: when we enter'd the Suburbs, the Lord Goring was Summoned, but returned an Answer not becoming a Gentleman: The Word of the Kings Forces at ye Fight was Charles, the ground they fought upon, Maries: Ours, God's – our help.

The Forces under the Command of Generall Fairfax engaged in ye Fight before Colchester, June 13. 1648. As also the names of the chief Commanders and persons of Quality of the Lord Gorings Forces engaged at that Fight.

Generall Fairfaxes *Forces engaged in that Fight.*
Part of the Generalls Regiment of Horse being 4 Troops, Commanded by Major Defbrough. *Of Col.* Whaleys *Regiment, 6 Troops, Commanded by himself. Of Col.* Fleetwoods, *5 Troops, Commanded by Major* Coleman. *Three Troops of Commissary Gen.* Iretons, *Commanded by Captain* Cecill. *Two Troops of Dragoons, Commanded by Captain* Freeman *and Captain* Barrington.

Of Foot.
Col. Barksteeds *Regiment Commanded by himself, confifting of 10 Companies, about 800 men. Col.* Needhams *Regiment, lately the Tower Regiment, Commanded by Col.* Needham, *being 7 Companies, and about 400 men. Part of Col.* Inglesby's *Regiment, of 4 Companies, Commanded by Capt.* Grimes, *320 men.*

Of the Effex Forces.
Col. Harlackendens *Regiment, of 4 Troops of Horse, Commanded by Major* Robert Sparrow; *and Captain* Turners *Troop of Dragoons. Sir Thomas* Hunniwoods *Regiment of Foot. Col.* Cooks *Regiment of Foot, both which said Regiments consisted of Auxiliaries, and Trained bands.*
    The County Forces of Effex *left to secure* Chelmsford *and* Maulden, *two considerable Pafses, left more Forces should resort from* London *to the Lord* Goring. *Colonel* Henry Mildmaies *Regiment of Horse, and two Troops of Dragoons. Part of Col.* Carew Mildmaies *Regiment of Foot, Commanded by Major* Bard.

The Suffolk Forces, who made good the Pafses over the River at Nailand, Stratford, *and* Cadaway, *left the Enemy should efcape towards* Suffolk *and* Norfolk, *were under the Command of Captain* Fifher, *Captain* Bradling, *and Captain* Sparrow, *besides the afsiftance which Capt.* Ball, *Capt.* Cox, *and the rest of the Sea Commanders gave to secure the River.*
    The Suffolk Forces that came afterwards to help befiege this Town.

Colonel Gourdons *Regiment of Horse.*
Of Foot Regiments.

Colonel Sir Thomas Barnadiftons, *Col.* Fothergils, *Col.* Harveys, *Col.* Bloises.

Of the Army that came up after the Fight.
Col. Scroop, *with 3 Troops of Horfe of his Regiment.*

The Lord Gorings *Forces engaged in that Fight.*

Of Horse.

Lord Gorings *Regiment, Lord* Capels *Regiment. Sir* William Comptons. *Col.* Slingſbies. *Col. Sir* Bernard Gascoignes. *Colonel* Hamonds. *Colonel* Culpeppers.

Of Foot.

Sir Charles Lucas *his Regiment. Sir* George Lifles *Regiment. Colonel* Tilleys *Regiment. Col.* Tewk *his Regiment. Col.* Farrs *Regiment. Colonel* Gilburds *Regiment Col. Sir* William Campions *Regiment, himself slain. Colonel* Burds *Regiment. Colonel* Bowmans *Regiment. Colonel* Chesters *Regiment.*

Colonels who had no Command of Regiments, yet aſsiſting at that Fight.
Earl Louborough, *Lord* Haftings, *Sir* William Leyton, *Colonel, taken Prisoner, and wounded, Colonel Sir* Richard Haftings, *Colonel* John Heath, *Colonel* Lee *of* Kent, *Colonel* Panton *wounded, Colonel* Cook *slain, Colonel Sir* Hugh Orelie, *Quarter maſter Gen. Col.* William Maxey, *Col.* Pitman, *Col.* Beal, *Lieu. Col.* Hatch *slain, Major* Jammot, *Adjutant Gen. Beſides divers Lieutenant Colonels and Majors who were aſsiſtants, but had no Commands.*

Wednesday 14 June.
Generall Fairfax *perceiving the Lord* Gorings *Forces would not ſtand the field, reſolved to sit down before the Town in order to a Siege (but being too few to Storm it) having not then nor when he first engaged, 1500 old Foot, and but about 1500 Horse, and two Troops of Dragoons, (beſides the 2 Regiments of the Trained Bands, under Col. Sir* Thomas Hunniwood, *and Col.* Cooke,) *the Lord* Gorings *Forces at that time being about 6000 Horse & Foot in Town, and the Town and Suburbs larger in Compas than Oxford, and would require 5000 men to Beſiege it; appointed* Lexden *in the road to* London *for the Head Quarter, where the greateſt Body was to lie, to prevent more aid for coming from* London *to the Lord* Goring, *and kept ſtrong Guards of Horse on* Cambridge *road, on the other side the River, that they might not eſcape Northward to joyn with Sir* Marmaduke Langdale, *leaving no place open to them, but towards the Sea, where they could not go far; and the same day Our Generall sent a Party of Horse to secure* Merſey Island, *to prevent the Kings Ships from coming into the River to relieve the Town; the Beſieged sent Col.* Tuke *with a ſtrong Party an hour after, but came too late.*

Thursday 15 June.

The Befiegeds Canon from the Royall Fort at St. Maries, *plaid very hard, killed severall of our men as they did the day before; some, as they were raifing the first Work called Fort Efsex, others as they were ftragling in the field.*

Friday 16 June.

Nothing of importance happened, 6.ut3 of Capt. Canons men killed with a Canon Bullet.

Saturday 17 June.

A Trumpet sent in about the Exchange of prisoners, & this day the Befieged got provifions out of Tendring Hundred, *which we could not prevent till ye* Suffolk *Forces march'd to our afsiftance.*

Sunday 18 June.

We took 2 of their Frigots, the one with 10, the other with 11 Guns. & this day Col. Ewers *came up with 6 Companies from* Chepstow Caftle: *The* Efsex *Foot under Sir* Tho. Hunniwood & Col. Cooke *endured many Canon fhot this day, and were very ready upon an Alarm.*

Munday 19 June.

The party of Horse sent from the Leaguer under Major Sparrow & Capt. Wallingford *engaged the* Kings *Forces at* Linton, *(coming to afsift the Lord* Goring,*) where Major* Muschampe & *others of the* Kings *Forces were flain, & Mafter* Reynolds, & *others taken prifoners, the reft (about 500.) disperst. This day a Trumpet came from ye Lord* Goring, *pretending to defire a Treaty of Peace.*

Tuefday 20 June.

Answer returned, if a generall Peace was intended, that then it was proper for the Parliament *to determine of that, and offered them in that anfwer Conditions, Viz. The Gentlemen & Officers to go beyond fea, and the Souldiers to go home, without prejudice.*

Wednefday 21 June.

The Befieged returned a fcornful anfwer, moving for a free-trade for the Townfmen.

148

Thursday 22 June.

A fmall Party of the Befieged fallied out to view a new Work (afterwards called Col. Ewers Fort)...............but were inftantly beaten in by Mufqueteers. Their Canon killed two men of ours. That day the Lord Goring fent a summons to the Suffolk Forces at Cattaway Bridge, Commanded by Capt. Fifher, & Capt. Brandling, to joyn with him, which they refufed Refolving ftill to adhere to the Parliament & Army.

Friday 23 June.

The Guns began this day to play from our new Battery, which much annoyed the Befieged at North bridge. Our Generall sent a Reply concerning his former offer, offering the same Conditions again to all in the Town, Except the Lord Goring, L.d Capell, and Sir Charles Lucas.

Saturday 24 June.

One of the Befiegeds Canoneers was killed. This day the Suffolk Forces advanced out of their own County, & took up their Quarters at upon Mile-end, over againft the North-gate, being about 2500 Horfe and Foot, leaving a guard at Cattaway, and Nayland, to fecure those pafses.

Sunday 25 June.

Nothing of importance.

Munday 26 June.

A party of Col. Barkfteeds Foot (the Befieged having drawn out near the Almes-house) beat them from ye Hedges, and from their Court of Guard, fired the Guard-houfe, and brought away the hour-glafs by which they ftood Centry.

Tuesday 27 June.

A Trumpeter went in with the Lady Campions Servant, with a Letter to her husband, for fhe did not believe he was flain.

Wednefday 28 June.

Chewed and Poysoned Bulletts taken from severall of the Befieged. Affidavit made by those Souldiers of ye Besieged who brought them out of Colchefter, that they were given out by the Lord Gorings fpeciall Command. Thefe Examinations were fent to ye Lord Goring, with this Mefsage from Our Generall, That his men fhould expect no Quarter hereafter, if they used such Bullits. This day early in the morning the Befieged with a party of Horfe, very boldly attempted our Horse Guards near St. Maries, fhot *a Scout, but were inftantly beaten back.*

Thurfday 29 June.
They killed some Hors & Foot of ours with their great Canon as they fhot against our men at ye making of Col. Barkfteeds Fort, fired at the House which was lately Sr. Harbottle Grimftons, & at night fired Mr Barringtons house, a party of the Befiegeds Horse advanced over the Bridge at Eaft-gate where Ambufcadoes being laid for them by our Dragoon's, Lieut. Col. Hatcher, & divers other Officers & Souldiers of the Befieged, upon their hafty advance were flain: none on our part.

Friday 30 June.
Exchange offered for Sir Will. Maffam, but refused.

Saturday 1 July.
Col. Whaley pofsest Grinfted Church.

Sunday 2 July.
Strong Guards kept that night to prevent the Befieged escape Northward, we having notice of their intention.

Monday 3, & Tuefday 4 July.
Little of moment happened, except a Porter, or Chamberlain coming from the Bell in Gratious ftreet stole into the Town, with Intelligence of the Earl of Hollands raifing an Army in, & about London for their relief.

Wednefday 5 July.
The Befieged sallied out with a ftrong party, Commanded by Sir George Lifle, furprifed our Guard at Eaft-bridge, and gained two Drakes, but advancing to ye Main Guard, were routed by Col. Whaleys horse, Commanded by Major Swallow; 19 flain on the place, the Drakes recovered and our former ground also; Lieut. Col. Wefton, Lieut. Col. Weeks, and 80 & odd prifoners were taken, moft of them sore cut for fhooting poisoned bullets (20 of them died the next day) On our part, we had slain Lieut. Col. Shambrooke, and some others of Col. Needhams Regiment, who were engaged, Capt. Moody on our fide wounded, & taken prifoner, and one Lieutenant & Enfign, & 40 private Soldiers of ours taken prisoners also.

Friday 7 July.
Col. Scroop sent from Leaguer by our Generall, with a Regiment of Horse, to engage

the Forces under ye Duke of Buckingham *and Earl of* Holland: *got into a body to raife ye Siege.*

Saturday 8 July.
News of Col. Roffiters *routing the* Pontifract *Forces at* Willoughby *field, where 3 Troops of the Army were engaged, & many of the men wounded;* Colonel Generall Sir Philip Mouncton, Major Generall Biron, *& divers Officers of quality taken prisoners by Colonell* Roffiter.

Sunday 9 July.
News of the Earl of Holland, *and Duke of* Buckinghams *being routed in* Surrey, *& of the Lord* Villiers *being flain by Sir* Michael Levefey, *& Major* Gibbons, *who Commanded a party of Horse of the Army.*

Monday 10 July.
Several of the Befieged came away to us; news came this day of the taking of 600 Horse in Northumberland, *& of Sir* Francis Ratcliff, *Col.* Tempeft, *Col.* Grey, *& other prisoners, taken by Col.* Lilburn.

Tuesday 11 July.
We had a Gunner & a Matrofse fhot as they were battering St. Maries *fteeple. News came this day of ye Earl of* Holland's *being taken prisoner by Col.* Scroop; *& Sir* Gilbert Gerrard, *& others of quality, & that Col.* Dalbeer *was flain, and their whole Force dispersed at S.* Needs *in* Huntingtonfhire.

Wednesday 12 & Thursday 13 July.
Little of moment happened, only M. John Afhburnham *offered in exchange for Sir* William Mafsam, *but not accepted; and this day the mefsenger who came to Our Generall with a Letter of the taking of* Waymer Caftle *in* Kent, *took his oppertunity, and carried it into* Colchester *to the Lord* Goring, *and took up arms there.*

Friday 14 July.
The new Battery being raised againft St. John's, *from the Lord* Lucas *house, 2 pieces of Canon plaid thence, made a breach in the wall: The Souldiers entred fell on immediately, drove the Befieged out of the first Court-yard into the second, & thence into ye Gatehouse, and the same day a ftrong party of Horfe & Foot fell upon the* Hieth, *& ftormed the Church, & took all the Guard therein prisoners, being about 70. and that night we poffest ourfelves of the* Hieth, *& a great part of the Suburbs,*

which much troubled ye Besieged: the Suffolk Foot did well in this service.

Saturday 15 July.

The Gate-house being a place very considerable, & mighty advantageous for us, Our Generall resolved to storm the same, though it had a strong work before it; whereupon 6 Souldiers, for 3 shillings apiece, undertook to throw in Grenadoes, and 20 men to carry Ladders for half a Crown apiece, & a Commanded party of Foot to storm, led on by Major Bescoe, which accordingly they did as soon as 8 piece of Canon had given fire upon the Besieged, and the Grenadoes did great execution, the Ladders were placed with much advantage, the Besieged much dismaied, forced to quit their works, & flie into the Gate-house, one Grenadoe kindled their Magazin, and blew up many of the Besieged, the rest were taken prisoners, and slain; the prisoners confest they were above a hundred in the Gate-house & work, and few of them could escape; 13 at one place were pulled out the next day from under the Rubbish. This night the Besieged indeavoured to escape with their horse, Commanded by Sir Bernard Gascoign, and past the River between the North-bridge & middle Mill, and had the Miller for their Guide, but ye Miller when he came into the Closes, ran away, and the Pioneers after him, and our Centinels giving fire, the Besieged retreated; The Suburbs was Fired in 6 or 7 places, which burnt in a most dreadfull manner all night long, that the Town might be seen almost as well by night as by day, so great was the flame.

And on Sunday the 16 other Streets were set on fire, with design to consume the whole Suburbs, but by the industry of the Inhabitants & Souldiers it was prevented. This day our Generall had certain Intelligence, That an Army of Scots under Duke Hamilton, had invaded the Kingdom, & joined the Cavaliers under Langdale.

Sunday 16 July.

Our Generall sent a Summons again to Surrender the Town: The Lord Goring, Lord Capell, & Sir Charles Lucas joyntly returned Answer (in writing,) under their hands to our Generall, That if the Trumpeter came any more with such a Summons, they would hang him up. The Conditions then offered to the Souldiers, was, Liberty, and Passes to go to their severall homes, submitting to the Authority of Parliament.

Munday 17 July.

Again more houses were fired towards ye North street, & other places. This day our Generall had certain News brought him of the Surrender of Pembrook Town & Castle, Langhorn, and Poyer submitting their lives to mercy.

152

Tuesday 18 July.
Their Horse again attempted to break through towards the North, but were beaten in again.

Wednefesday 19 July.
Seventeen of the Befieged this day came over to us, and their Horse were all drawn this day
into the Caftle-yard, & a certain number out of every Troop was chosen to be killed; and there were told in the Caftle Baily, 700 horse belonging to the Souldiers.

Thursday 20 July.
They killed their horses; one Butcher ran away rather than he would do it. The Befieged at night drew out their Horse at 12 of the clock, and afterwards at 2 of the clock in the morning to efcape, but our men were in such readinefs they durft not advance.

Friday 21July.
News came of Captain Batten's Revolt to the Revolted Ships, deferting the Parliament, and turning to the King.

Saturday 22 July.
Severall Souldiers ran from the Befieged much complaining of their Diet in horse-flefh, & a Trumpeter was this day sent in again to expediate ye Exchange of Sir Willm. Maffam, for Mr. Afhburnham, but ye Befieged refused it, as also to admit of ye exchange of the reft of ye Committee, though they had Gentlemen of very good rank offered for them (quality for quality) in exchange.

Sunday 23 July.
The Befieged roafted a horse near the North-bridge to make the Souldiers merry at ye entrance into fuch Diet; this day our Generall had Intelligence of Col. Lamberts engagement with the Scots, near Appleby: where above 100 Scots were flain, Col. Harrifon & others on our part wounded.

Munday 24 July, Nothing of moment.

Tuefday 25 July.
The Befieged had a hot Alarm round the Town about 12 at night, and a partie in the meane time fired the Middle Mill with the lofs of three men, and cut off

a fluce, but the fire did not take, so the defign proved ineffectuall at that time; at the same time we fhot 20 Arrows, (with papers of advertisement offered) into the Town, to undeceive the Souldiers; acquainting them with what Conditions were offered them, and fhall ftill be made good unto them, if they come out: which coming to some of their knowledge above 200 came out by that day 7. night.

Wednefday 26 July, *Nothing of moment.*

Thursday 27 July.
A Troop of the Lord Capells fallied out, and took 3 or 4 men as they were working upon the Line near St. Botolphs, and wounded one miferably, being a Country Souldier & but a fpectator.

Friday, Saturday & Sunday 28. 29. & 30.
Nothing of moment.

Munday 31 July.
In the night about 20 of them with Spades, 6 only having Mufkets, paft the first Centinell as friends, faying, they were come to make an end of the work where they wrought the night before, but were fired upon at the second guard, had a Lieutenant slain, and retreated, and took a Serjeant with them prifoner.

Tuesday Auguft 1.
A Cornet, Quartermafter, Corporall, and one Trooper came away with their horfes.

Wednefday 2. & Thursday the third Auguft.
There came severall Souldiers from the Befieged, much complayning of their ill diet with horseflefh, and said it was attended with Gentlewomen in white Gownes & black hoods (meaning Maggots) so that they could not eat it, & that it had brought many of them to the flux.

Friday 4. Saturday 5. & Sunday 6 Auguft. *Nothing recorded.*

Monday 7 Auguft.
Nothing of moment hapned: this day it was refolved at a full Councill of War; to proceed by way of Approaches in order to a Storm.

Tuesday 8. Wednesday 9. & Thurfday 10.
Nothing recorded.

Friday 11Auguft.
Nothing of note. This night 30 houfes were burnt.

Saturday 12. Sunday13. & Munday 14.
Nothing recorded.

Tuesday 15 Auguft.
Many men came over this day from the Befieged, & the poorer sort of people began to rise for want of bread.

Wednesday 16 Auguft.
They rise in great Numbers, and come to the Lord Gorings Quarters, some bringing their Children ftarved to death, they crying out, so long as Horseflefh, Dogs, and Cats were to be had, they did not complain. This day the Mayor of Colchester sent a Letter to the Gen. That the Inhabitants might come out, for that they had no provifion, it being all feised by the Souldiers. Our Generall returned anfwer. He pittied their condition, but to grant that, was to make the Town hold out longer, and did not ftand with his truft to permit it. This day we had the news of the killing & difpersing the Princes forces by some Horfe and Foot of the Army, commanded by Col. Rich, near Deale; and also of the regaining of Tinmouth Caftle by Sir Arthur Hafelrigg.

Thurfday 17 Auguft.
The Lord Goring, Lord Capell, and Sir Charles Lucas, who before threatened to hang our Trumpeter if he came any more with a Meffage for a Party, desired Our Generall they might send to the King's Forces, and if they had not relief within 20 days, they would then Treat. Answer was returned by Our Gen. That he hop'd in much lefs time than 20 days, to have the Town without Treaty. All things are preparing in Order to a ftorm.

Friday 18 August.
No action but preparation for ftorm.

Saturday 19 Auguft.
The Befieged fent for a Treaty to surrender.

Sunday 20 Auguſt.

The Generall returned an answer to their offer for a Treaty. That all Souldiers & Officers under the degree of a Captain, (excepting such as have deserted the Army since the 10 of May last) ſhall have Paſſes to go to their severall homes; and all Captaines,and Superior Officers, with Lords, and Gentlemen to mercie.

Munday 21 Auguſt.

The Beſieged turned out of the Town in the night, many men, women, & children, but the next morning took them in again.

Tueſday 22 Auguſt.

The Beſieged sent out Major Sheffield one of the Committee that was prisoner in Colchester, that they would surrender upon honourable conditions, and desire to know the meaning of ye word mercie. This day the news of routing the Scotiſh army came, which we sent into the Town.

FINIS.

Printed and Sold by Tho: Witham at the
Golden Ball in Long Lane near

West Smithfield   LONDON

Selected Biographies

BRADSHAW, John 1602-59

President of the High Court of Justice, which condemned King Charles I. He studied law at Gray's Inn and attained a fair practice. When the King's trial was determined upon, Bradshaw was appointed president of the court; his stern and unbending deportment at the trial did not disappoint expectation. Afterwards he opposed Cromwell and the Protectorate, and was in consequence deprived of the chief justiceships of Chester. On the death of Cromwell he became Lord President of the Council and died in 1659. At the Restoration his body was exhumed and hung on a gibbet with those of Cromwell and Ireton.

BUCKINGHAM, George Villiers II Duke of 1628-87

English courtier. Born 30 January 1628, he was a son of the first Duke whom he succeeded in August 1628. Brought up with the children of Charles I he served on the Royalist side in the Civil War. In 1651 his estates were sequestrated, but in 1657 he married the daughter of the parliamentary general Fairfax, to whom most of his estates had been assigned under the Commonwealth.

After Clarendon's fall, which was largely due to him, he was the most influential of the King's advisors. In 1668 he was a chief member of the Cabel ministry, but after attacking Arlington in 1673 he lost favour. Buckingham died on 16 April 1687 and the Dukedom became extinct. Satirised as Zimri in Drydon's Absalom and Achitophel, he was a wit, a writer of verses, and a dabbler in chemistry.

CAPEL, Arthur 1600-49

English Royalist and son of Sir Henry Capel. He was born about 1600 and was nephew to the Earl of Manchester, who was a leading parliamentarian. Disgusted with Parliamentarian extremism, he became an ardent Royalist.

He elected member for Hertfordshire in the Short Parliament and the Long Parliament of 1640. He fought for the King during the Civil War, escorted Queen Henrietta to Paris helped Charles to escape from Hampton Court and, in August 1648, surrendered to Fairfax at Colchester.

During the Civil Warhe fought bravely as one of the Royalist generals in the west in the engagements at Bristol, Exeter and Taunton.

He was raised to the peerage by Charles I in 1641 as Lord Capel of Hadham, Hertfordshire and he connived in the King's flight from Hampton Court to the Isle of Wight in 1648.

After the Siege of Colchester he was imprisoned in the Tower of London, from where he escaped (one of the very few persons to do so), before being betrayed by a waterman and recaptured.

He was tried and beheaded 9 March 1649 at Westminster Hall and buried at Much Hadham.

CHARLES I 1600-1649

Son of James I of England, he was born at Dunfermline on 19 November 1600. On the death of his elder brother Henry in 1612, he became his father's heir and in 1616 was made Prince of Wales. He succeeded to the throne in 1625 when he married Henrietta Maria of France.

From 1625-29 Charles was engaged in a ceaseless contest with his parliaments. He dissolved Parliament in 1629 and ruled without one for eleven years, raising money by every possible device.

In 1639 an attempt, at the instigation of Archbishop Laud, to impose an Anglican liturgy upon Scotland united the Scots in armed opposition. The Kingís financial resources were exhausted so, in 1640, advised by his chief supporter, Strafford, he summoned the Short Parliament which refused supplies and was dissolved. In the same year he summoned the Long Parliament by which Strafford was arrested and executed and Charles was forced to consent to various reforms. Following an attempt to arrest five members of Parliament, in January 1642, Charles left London and the Civil War began in August.

In the first two campaigns, success lay with the Royalists, but in 1644 the Parliamentary army defeated them at Marston Moor, and in 1645 the cause of Charles received its deathblow at Naseby. Charles surrendered to the Scots who handed him over to the English Parliament. He was finally tried for treason and beheaded on 30 January 1649.

CROMWELL, Oliver 1599-1658

Lord Protector of the Commonwealth of England, Scotland and Ireland, he was born at Huntingdon, 25 April 1599. His father, Robert Cromwell, who represented the borough of Huntingdon in the Parliament of 1593, was a younger son of Sir Henry Cromwell who was knighted by Queen Elizabeth.

The first really authentic fact in Cromwell's biography is his leaving school at Huntingdon and entering Sidney Sussex College, Cambridge on 23 April 1616. On the death of his father in 1617 he returned home and later in married Elizabeth, daughter of Sir James Bourchier, in 1620. In 1628 he was elected Member of Parliament for Huntingdon, to which he was returned on the dissolution in 1629.

In 1631 he went with his family to a farm that he had taken at St. Ives, and in 1636 to Ely, where he had inherited a property worth nearly £500 a year.

During the Short and Long Parliaments Cromwell represented Cambridge. In the summer of 1642 he was actively engaged in raising and drilling volunteers for the Parliamentary party as a result of the impending struggle with King Charles I.

When the Civil War broke out Cromwell organized his own district and at Edgehill commanded a troop of horse. He then raised his Ironsides (cavalry troopers) who showed their quality at Marston Moor, and under his command the New Model Army was victorious at Naseby. In March 1648 Cromwell crushed the Welsh rising in Pembrokeshire and later defeated the Scots at Preston.

A member of the Rump Parliament, he was one of three who signed the warrant for the King's execution. Affairs in Ireland demanding his presence, he was appointed Lord Lieutenant and Commander-in-Chief; of the Parliamentary forces. In 1653 Cromwell dissolved the Rump Parliamentary and formed a Council of State. After the dismissal of the short-lived Barebones Parliament he was declared Lord Protector with almost unlimited powers. He died on 3 September 1658.

FARRE, Colonel Henry, 1603

English soldier born in 1603 and a Captain of the Essex trained band in 1634. In 1642 he, along with others, protested against Dutch officers being brought into the regiment on account of their greater military experience. He was committed to the custody of the Serjeant-at-Arms of the House of Commons, and removed from the office of Deputy Lieutenant and membership of the County Committee in September 1643. He later made his peace with the authorities and was restored to the rank of lieutenant colonel in the Earl of Warwickís Regiment of Militia. In May 1648, a petition from the county was presented to Parliament asking that an arrangement should be entered into with the King and that the army should be disbanded. The County Committee was ordered to meet at Chelmsford on 4 June to deal with the situation, but with popular feeling running so high the crowd, led by Colonel Farre, made them prisoners. Shortly afterwards Farre went over to Goring with 400 of his trained band. Matthew Carter in his account of the Siege of Colchester in 1648 says that, on the surrender of the town Colonel Farre escaped, but was retaken. At the time of the Restoration Farre was commissioned as lieutenant of a Company at Landguard Fort, under Charles Rich, fourth Earl of Warwick and the

Governor of the Fort. On 16 November 1664, Farre himself was appointed Governor of Landguard Fort, a position he held until his Company was transferred to Yarmouth in 1667.

FAIRFAX, Thomas, 3rd Baron 1612-71

An English soldier, Thomas Fairfax was the son of the second Baron, Ferdinando 1584-1648. He was born at Denton, Yorkshire on 17 January 1612 and educated at St. John's College, Cambridge.

Gaining his military experience in the Netherlands under Sir Horace Vere, one of the de Veres of Hedingham, whose daughter he later married. He was Knighted by Charles I in 1640 for his services against the Scots.

During the Civil War in 1644 he served under his father Ferdinando at Marston Moor, and in 1645 he was appointed Commander-in-Chief of the of the Parliamentary army. Under his leadership, the army was successful in numerous campaigns before the Royalists were finally defeated

He was one of the judges appointed to try Charles I but he refused to sit, and in 1650 he resigned as head of the army. In 1659 he helped General Monck to restore Charles II to the throne, and in the following year was elected M.P. for Yorkshire, a position he held until his death in November 1671.

GASCOIGNE, Sir Bernard 1614-87

Born Bernadino Guasconi; a Florentine, who gained his military experience in Italy and Germany. Following the surrender of the Siege of Colchester in 1648, Sir Bernard, along with Sir Charles Lucas and Sir George Lisle, were sentenced to death by General Fairfax, fearing that the execution of this nobleman could possibly threaten the long-term future relationship with another foreign power, the decision was made to grant him his life.

In 1669, Sir Bernard Gascoigne revisited Colchester in the company of Cosimo, the Duke of Tuscany, and showed him the site where his friends Sir Charles Lucas and Sir George Lisle were executed.

GORING, Lord George 1583-1663

Lord Goring was educated at Sidney Sussex College, Cambridge (where Cromwell also studied), he was instrumental in arranging the marriage of Charles I to the French princess Henrietta Maria. He helped to raise money for the King in the early part of the Civil War, for which he was created Earl of Norwich, but took no active part in the fighting at this stage. After the Siege of Colchester he was tried by Parliament and acquitted, supposedly on the casting vote of William Lenthall, Speaker of the House. He died in London and is buried in Westminster Abbey. His son, also known as Lord Goring, fought at Marston Moor in 1644 and went into exile after his unsuccessful defence of Portsmouth. Parliament refused to recognise his title as the Earl of Norwich and continued to use his earlier style of Lord Goring. This title, however, passed to his son on his father's elevation to the peerage, hence the confusion.

GRIMSTON, Sir Harbottle 1603-1685

Judge and Speaker of the House of Commons and second son of Sir Harbottle Grimston, a puritan gentleman who was created a Baronet in 1612.

Born at Bradfield Hall in Essex and educated at Emmanuel College in Cambridge, Sir Harbottle entered the Lincolnís Inn and was called to the Bar. On 16 April 1629 he married Mary Croke, the daughter of Sir George Croke. In 1628 he became a Member of Parliament for the constituency of Harwich, and in 1634 he became a Recorder of the town.

In 1637 he bought a house in Colchester which had been built on the site of a house belonging to the former Crouched Friars, and there he raised a large family. In 1638 he was elected Recorder of Colchester, which borough he represented in the first parliament of 1640, and the Long parliament. He resigned the recorder-ship of Colchester in 1649 and retired to his Bradfield home to devote more time to the education of his children, with whom he also travelled for a time on the continent. In 1656, however, he was returned to Parliament for the county of Essex and in 1660 he became Speaker of the House of Commons when he had the honour of welcoming Charles II.

HENRIETTA Maria 1609-69 Queen of Charles I

Henrietta was born in Paris on 25 November 1609 and was the first child of Henry IV of France. She married Charles I of England in 1624 after he had failed to secure a Spanish bride. The Queen was fond of gaiety and extravagance, but her partiality for the Roman Catholics governed almost all that she did in English politics, and her activities prior to the outbreak of the Civil War did much to fan the flame of discontent. In 1644, she left England and never saw Charles again. She returned to England in 1660 lived for some time at Somerset House, London. She died at Colombes, near Paris, on 31 August 1669.

IRETON, Henry 1611-51

English soldier. Born at Attenborough, near Nottingham, Ireton joined the

Parliamentary forces during the Civil War and was soon associated with Cromwell in Lincolnshire. He served at Marston Moor, Newbury and Naseby. In Parliament, Ireton drafted the Heads of the Proposals and strove to reunite the moderate men of both parties. When this failed he took an active part in the renewal of the Civil War and was one of the King's judges, signing his death warrant. In 1646 he married Cromwell's daughter Bridget, thus increasing his influence in the high councils of the army and Parliament. In 1650 Ireton was made Lord Deputy of Ireland, from where he died of the plague in November 1651. He was buried in the Westminster Abbey in 1652, but after the Restoration his remains were disinterred, hanged, and burned at Tyburn.

LUCAS, Sir Charles 1613 -1648

Youngest son of Sir Thomas Lucas whose forebears had bought St. John's Abbey after the Dissolution. He seems to have been of an overbearing disposition, and of dissolute habits. In 1643 he was appointed Commander-in-Chief of all the Royalist forces raised in Essex and Suffolk. In 1644 he was taken prisoner at Marston Moor, but was later exchanged for a Parliamentarian officer. He was captured again at Stow-on-the-Wold in 1645 and was imprisoned in the church there. He was later released on parole on the condition that he would not again bear arms against Parliament. He was present during the Siege of Colchester in 1648, and following the town's surrender he was executed by the command of Sir Thomas Fairfax, General of the Parliamentary Army.

LISLE, Sir George (died 1648)

Son of a Hertfordshire bookseller Lisle received his military experience in the Netherlands. During the English Civil War he fought at both battles of Newbury where his bravery was conspicuous. He was captured after the fall of Farringdon, near Oxford, in 1646 and later released on parole. Lisle was also present at the Siege of Colchester in 1648 and following the town's surrender, shared the same fate as Sir Charles Lucas.
He was buried alongside his companion in St. Giles' Church, Colchester.

LAUD, William 1573-1645

William Laud was born at Reading in 1573 where he received an elementary education before attending St. John's College, Oxford. He was admitted a Fellow of the college in 1593 and in 1608 became chaplain to Niele, Bishop of Rochester. In 1617 he became king's chaplain accompanying James I on a visit to Scotland.

On the accession of Charles I, Laud was nominated Bishop of Bath and Wells, a career move which was to lead to his becoming Archbishop of Canterbury in 1633. His High Church policy in support of Charles I, and his persecution of the Puritans, aroused bitter opposition from numerous quarters, and his attempt to impose the use of the Prayer Book on the Scots precipitated the English Civil War. He was impeached by Parliament in 1640 and imprisoned in the Tower of London. He was later condemned and beheaded on Tower Hill on 10 January, 1645.

RUPERT, Prince 1619-82

German Prince and son of the Elector Palatine, Frederick V. and Elizabeth daughter of James I of England. Rupert was born at Prague in December 1619 and was to later fight on the Protestant side during the Thirty Year's War. He came to England in 1642 and fought for the Royalist cause at Worcester, Edgehill, Marston Moor and Naseby, proving himself a dashing if somewhat erratic leader of cavalry. He commanded the Royalist fleet between 1648 and 1650, during which time most of his ships were destroyed by Admiral Robert Blake, off Malaga. After the Restoration he saw further naval service against the Dutch. Prince Rupert died on 29 November 1682.

Glossary

Accompt,	an account
Accoutered,	to furnish with dress or equipments, especially that of a soldier
Ailsford,	Alresford, Kent
Ambufcade,	to lie in ambush
Anglia Rediviva,	article written by the Rev. Spragg, Chaplain to Sir Thomas Fairfax on the Conduct of the Parliament Army under Fairfax
Apostatism,	to abandon or renounce one's religious faith or moral allegiance – to become an apostate
Appurtenances,	usually certain rights associated with a tenancy – items or accessories associated with a particular activity or way of living
Barracadoed,	barracaded
Basely,	with contemptible cowardice - dishonorably
Belial,	the devil
Burthan,	a load, duty, responsibility etc
Calverin,	[Culverin] long barrelled cannon 4,500 Ibs
Cannoneers,	artillary Soldiers
Cattaway,	Cattawade, near Manningtree
Chirgeons,	a surgeon, working with the hand
Clamors,	loud noises, people shouting
Cloaths,	clothes
Cockertrices,	serpent said to kill by its mere glance, and to be hatched from a cock's egg [Basilisk]
Cornets,	Military rank between Lieutenant and Sergeant
Demicannon,	a type of cannon – usually half the size of a full piece 6,000 Ibs
Distempers,	disturbances, troubles etc
Divers,	various / several
Doublet,	a close fitting garment, covering the body from the neck to a little below the waist
Drake,	a small type of cannon
Ensign,	Military rank between Lieutenant and Sergeant
Flanker,	fortification to protect a flank

Forlorns,	soldiers picked to begin an attack, many of which would not survive
Grenadoes,	Grenades
Halbert,	a weapon with a long shaft having a steel pointed head, and a steel crosspiece with a cutting edge
Hambleteers,	Tower Hamlet Regiment, Militia
Heavy Berthen,	possibly meaning heavy burden
Hieth,	Hythe
Immeriting,	undeserving
Impaneled,	to enlist or enrol on a panel or jury
Lathe,	a former administration District in Kent
Leaguer,	a member of a league or alliance
Machivilian,	astute, cunning, intriguing, etc,
Matrosses,	a soldier next in rank below a gunner who acted as assistant or mate
Musquet,	light gun with long barrel
Militia,	an organisation containing men enlisted for service in emergency only
Nailand,	[Nayland], Suffolk
Pinnace,	a small light vessel, generally two masted and schooner rigged
Remonstrance,	a forceful protest
Saker,	a small cannon, 2,500 lbs
Sally,	to make an attack or advance
Shavers,	Soldiers armed with Billhooks and Scythes
Sheergate,	[Scheregate]
Trained Bands,	a trained company of soldiers, militia etc
Turkishly,	in the Turkish manner or way (i.e. cruel, savage, barbarous)
Vanish into Stink,	slang for fuss, furore
Vassallage,	under the protection of another who is his or her feudal lord
Warmer,	[Walmer] Castle, Kent
Wooden-Horse,	Military instrument of punishment

Select Bibliography

There are many documents and records are available concerning 'The Siege of Colchester', we have however, listed below a selective guide to some further reading, primarily of books and periodicals that are readily available at Record Offices and Libraries (local studies section).

Appleby, D., 'Our Fall Our Fame: The Life and Times of Sir Charles Lucas 1613-1648' (1996)

Bell, R.E. Editor., 'The Fairfax Correspondence (1849)

Boustred, R.E., Last Stand for the King, Colchester Borough Council (1974)

Carter, M., A True Relation of That Honorable, Though Unfortunate Expedition of Kent, Essex, and Colchester, in 1648 J. Fenno (1789)

Clarke, D.T., The Siege of Colchester 1648, Colchester Borough Council (1974)

Crake, E.E., 'The Royalist Brothers', a tale of the siege of Colchester, SPCK (1908)

Defoe, D.A., A Tour Through the Eastern Counties, first published 1724, republished 1949, republished by East Anglian magazine Limited, 1984

Downing, T. and Millman, M., 'Civil War' London (1998)

Hodgson, T., 'The Siege of Colchester', Colchester Borough Council and Jarrold Publishing (1998)

Howard, M., Suffering during the Siege of Colchester, 1648 (1997)

Jarmin, A.M., 'The Story of the Siege of Colchester' 1648, Journal British Archaeological Association (1919)

Markham, C.R., 'The Siege of Colchester' Archaelogical Journal Vol. 34 (1877)

Morant, P., The History and Antiquities of Colchester (1748)

Neale, K., 'Essex in History' Chichester, West Sussex (1997)

Pitkin Guide., 'The Civil War' 1642-51

Townsend, G.F., 'The Siege of Colchester' or An Event of the Civil War, A.D. 1648, SPCK c.1880

Wire, W., 'Colchester Teares, 1648' Reprinted by John Bawtree (1843)

Wright, F., 'The Siege of Colchester', Wright & Sons (1899)

Index of Persons

Penroy, William 124
Peyton, Thomas 34
Pitman, *Colonel* 147
Pits, *Captain* 103
Portlar, Mrs. 122
Potter, Vincent 124
Powell, *Lieutenant Colonel* 103
Pride, Thomas 124
Prince, James 124
Pulliston, Joseph 124

R.

Rainsborow, Thomas, *Colonel* 24,
  29, 80, 100, 112, 119
Ratcliff, *Sir* Francis 151
Rawlins, *Lieutenant Colonel* 61
Reynolds, *Master* 148
Rich, *Colonel* 155
Richmond *Duke of* 38
Ricot's, *Sir* Peter 14
Rivers, John 9
Roberts, *Sir* Edward 34
Roberts, *Sir* John 31
Robinson, Mr. 122
Roe, Owen 124
Rossiter, *Colonel* 151
Rot, *Sir* William 124
Roysard, George 122

S.

Saltinghall, Sir R. 124
Saunders, Tho. 124
Savine, *Justice of the Peace* 2, 3
Sawyer, *Colonel* 103
Scarrow, *Major* 103
Scot, *Lady* Katherine 83
Scroop, *Colonel* 150, 151
Scudamore, *Colonel* 63
Senyar, Crefield 122

Shambrooke, *Lieutenant Colonel* 150
Sheffield, *council of war* 89
Sheffield, *Major* 156
Sheffield, Samp 124
Shepperd, Matthew 124
Shipman, *Sir* Abraham 100, 103
Short, John, *carpenter of Swallow* 30
Shut, Richard 124
Simson, John 122
Sir Henry H—— 23
Sir *(T- - - T)* 11
Slingsbie, *Colonel* 147
Smight, William 122
Smith, *Captain* 103
Smith, *Lieutenant Colonel* 103
Smith, *Major* 103
Smith, Solomon 124
Snellgrave, *Captain* 104
Sparrow, *Captain* 100, 146, 148
Sparrow, Richard 124
Sparrow, Robert, *Major* 146
Spence, William 124
Spragg, *The Rev. Chaplain to*
  Sir Thomas Fairfax 119
Stephens, *Captain* 104
Steel, *Sergeant* 3, 125
Steward, *Colonel* 63
Stone, Richard 121
Street, Richard 121
Stone, John 124
Strut, *Sir* Dennard 103
Summer, *Major* 43
Swallow, *Major* 150
Swan, *Lieutenant* 23
Syliard, Thomas 9

T.

Taylor, Daniel 124
Taylor, Silvanus 124

Index of Places

Index of Subjects